THE NAIADS

Library and Archives Canada Cataloguing in Publication information is available upon request.

ISBN-13: 978-1-77478-200-2

Copyright © 2025 Engen Books

All images © 2025 Kelly Bastow

Refuge, Singing Lessons, Fathom, Demi-Gods, Bodies of Water, Cathedrals in Atlantis, The Steeple of the Sea Witch, Pickings, Seep, and, Sodden Women © 2025 Hannah Jenkins

Poem #2, Poem #5, Poem #6, Poem #8, Poem #12, Poem #15, Poem #16, Poem #21, Poem #22, Poem #24 © 2025 Samm Joyy

The Girl who Never Stopped Bleeding, Beyond the Sea, Black Moon Lilith, Girl vs. Shark: A Tragedy in Three Acts, Honestly and Deeply, Everything Nice, Girl's Girl, Le bal des folles, Old Wives' Tale, The Fly Catcher © 2025 Krysta Fitzpatrick

NO PART OF THIS BOOK MAY BE REPRODUCED OR TRANSMITTED IN ANY FORM OR BY ANY MEANS, ELECTRONIC OR MECHANICAL, INCLUDING PHOTOCOPYING AND RECORDING, OR BY ANY INFORMATION STORAGE OR RETRIEVAL SYSTEM WITHOUT WRITTEN PERMISSION FROM THE COPYRIGHT HOLDER, EXCEPT FOR BRIEF PASSAGES QUOTED IN A REVIEW.

This book is a work of fiction. Names, characters, places and incidents are products of each author's imagination or are used fictitiously. Any resemblance to actual events or locales or persons living or dead is entirely coincidental.

Distributed by:
Engen Books
www.engenbooks.com
submissions@engenbooks.com

First mass market paperback printing: September 2025
Second mass market paperback printing: May 2026
Cover Image: © 2025 Kelly Bastow

CONTENTS

Refuge
Hannah Jenkins.................004

Poem #2
Samm Joyy......................006

Girl vs. Shark: A Tragedy in Three Acts
Krysta Fitzpatrick..............007

Singing Lessons
Hannah Jenkins.................008

Poem #5
Samm Joyy......................010

Poem #6
Samm Joyy......................011

Fathom
Hannah Jenkins.................012

Poem #8
Samm Joyy......................014

Demi-Gods
Hannah Jenkins.................016

Bodies of Water
Hannah Jenkins.................018

Beyond the Sea
Krysta Fitzpatrick..............020

Poem #12
Samm Joyy......................022

Cathedrals in Atlantis
Hannah Jenkins.................024

The Girl Who Never Stopped Bleeding
Krysta Fitzpatrick..............026

Poem #15
Samm Joyy......................029

Poem #16
Samm Joyy......................030

Black Moon Lilith
Krysta Fitzpatrick..............032

Pickings
Hannah Jenkins.................034

Honestly and Deeply
Krysta Fitzpatrick..............035

Everything Nice
Krysta Fitzpatrick..............036

Poem #21
Samm Joyy......................039

Poem #22
Samm Joyy......................040

Girl's Girl
Krysta Fitzpatrick..............042

Poem #24
Samm Joyy......................044

Seep
Hannah Jenkins.................046

Le bal des folles
Krysta Fitzpatrick..............048

Sodden Women
Hannah Jenkins.................050

Old Wives' Tale
Krysta Fitzpatrick..............052

The Steeple of the Sea Witch
Hannah Jenkins.................054

The Fly Catcher
Krysta Fitzpatrick..............056

Refuge

Bury me breathing
in these clear water graves
Amid the faint pops of kelp
pressed tight between fingers,
with saltwater ear drums and
bits of fish scales suspended
in the waves like dust

No one has spoken here in centuries
Every movement, quiet and weighted
Water slicing like skin beneath a scalpel

Fetch me after the world's last shipwreck
Perhaps then I'll be ready for living
and the sharp sound of doors,
the shrieks and the bustle,
the ceaseless tasks
and tasks and
tasks of it all

Hannah Jenkins

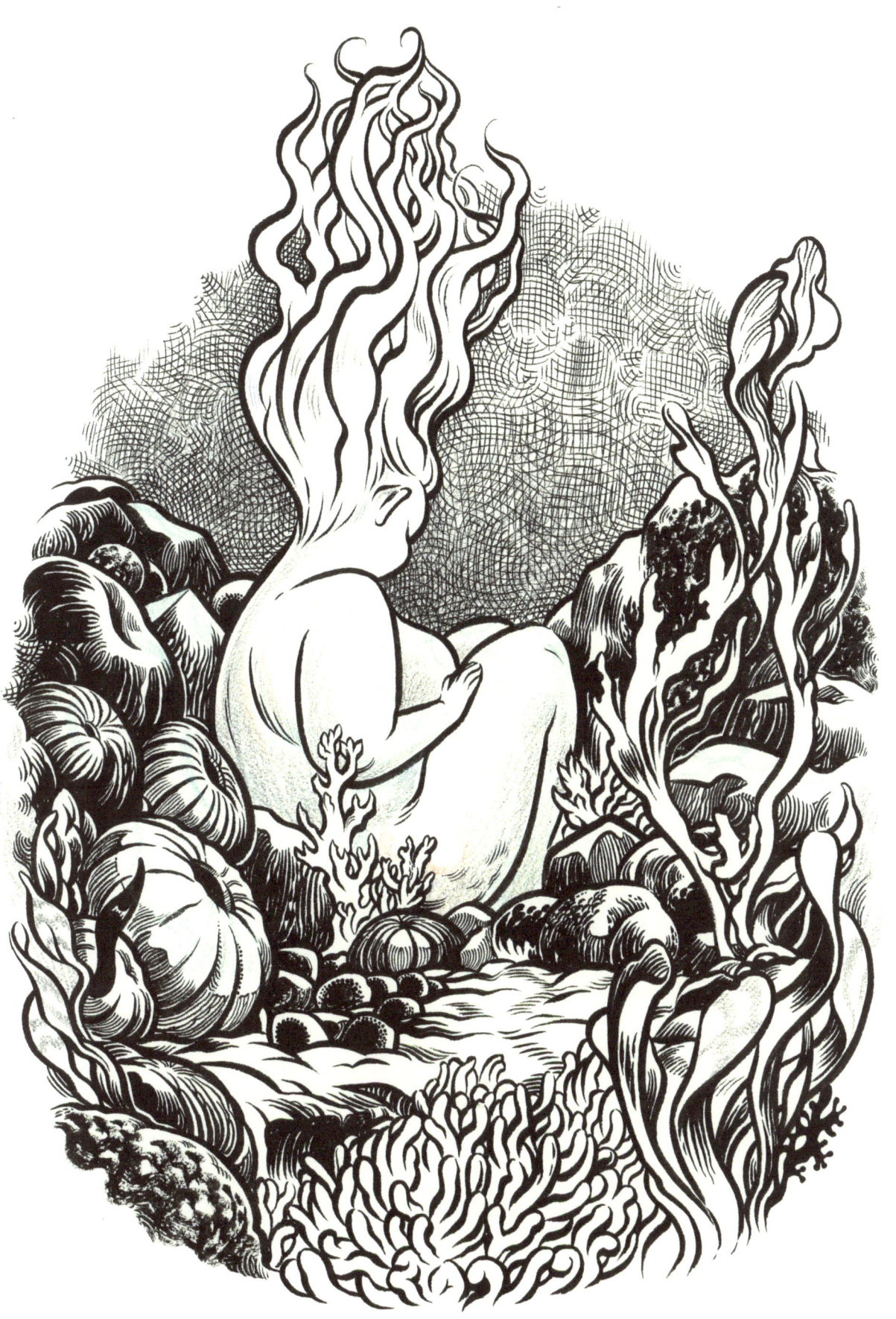

I slide my nails along the floorboards
Like I did your back
Leaving a piece of me
Everywhere I go

I refuse to be forgotten
Act like someone
You've never known
Like these floor boards
I have supported many souls
And yours was the one
That caused me to crack

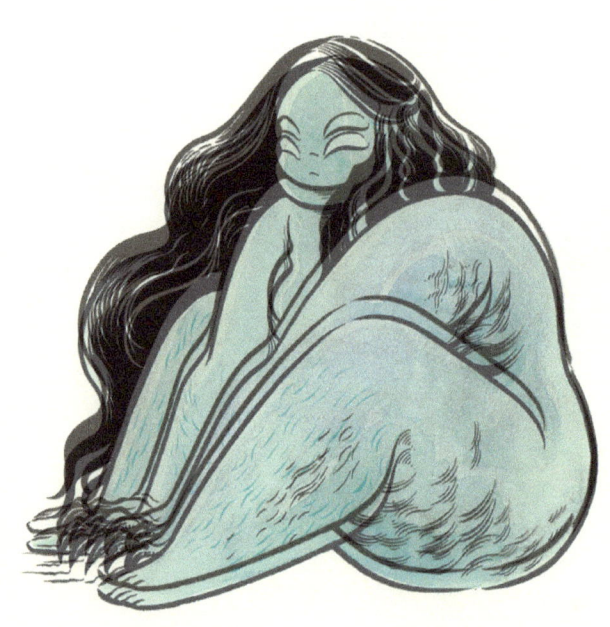

Girl vs. Shark: A Tragedy in Three Acts

Act One:
The skin of a female shark can be twice as thick as that of a male.

Which would be beneficial to the females if they knew what it was like to be called a slut, a prude, a tease, or a bitch.

Female humans are often told they must develop a thick skin to survive,

but, alas, a girl is not a shark.

Act Two:
Female sharks typically have larger, sharper teeth than the males.

Which would probably deter male sharks from constantly telling them that they would look prettier if they smiled.

Female humans have tiny teeth that invoke no terror in our male counterparts. Our smiles lack menace, so they keep requesting them.

Alas, a girl is not a shark.

Act Three:
Female sharks tend to be larger than male sharks.

This, of course, probably means that no female shark ever feels a need to clutch her keys between her knuckles as she swims home at night.

Few female humans have the luxury of safety in their size, so, we cling to our keys and hope, not that nothing bad will happen, but that whatever bad happens will at least be survivable,

because, alas, a girl is not a shark.

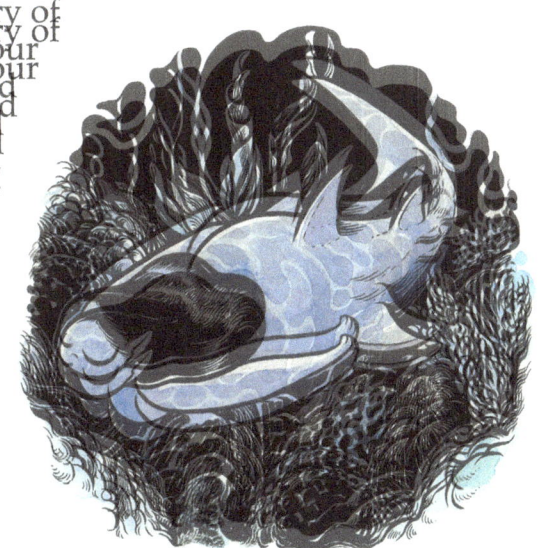

Krysta Fitzpatrick

Singing Lessons

We are all animals — you and I
and the frogs and the mermaids

We are all brief, half real
chunks of carbon and dew
waiting for a midnight chorus

The same notes
situated in different vocal chords
The same lightning
shooting across dual minds

We are but two attempts at a morning
staring back at one another

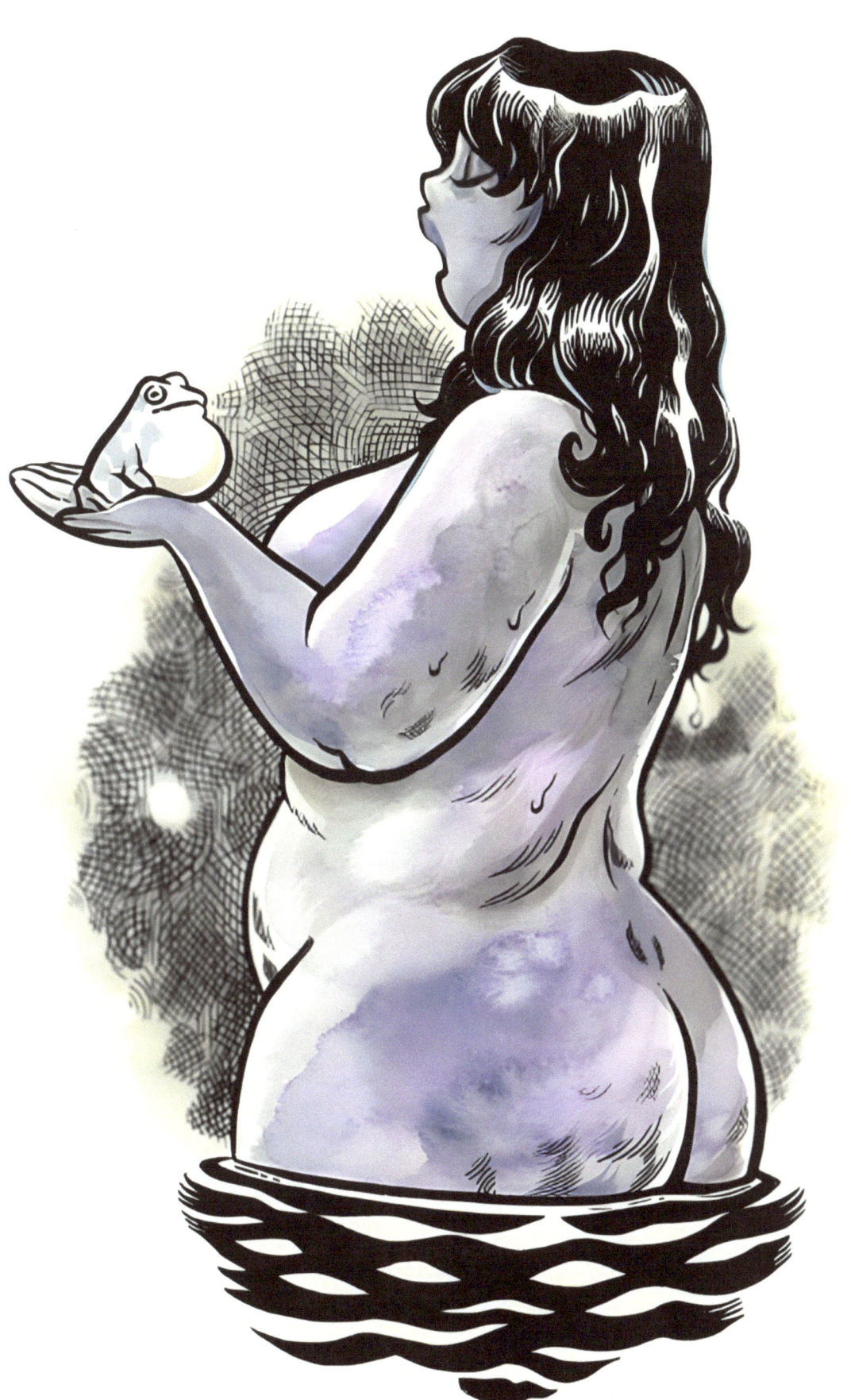

A woman with so many words
Filling the air – the void
With pointless conversation
To delay the silence
Talking at anyone who will listen
Or pretend to
Just for a moment
Of distraction
From all the words
She cannot speak

Samm Joyy

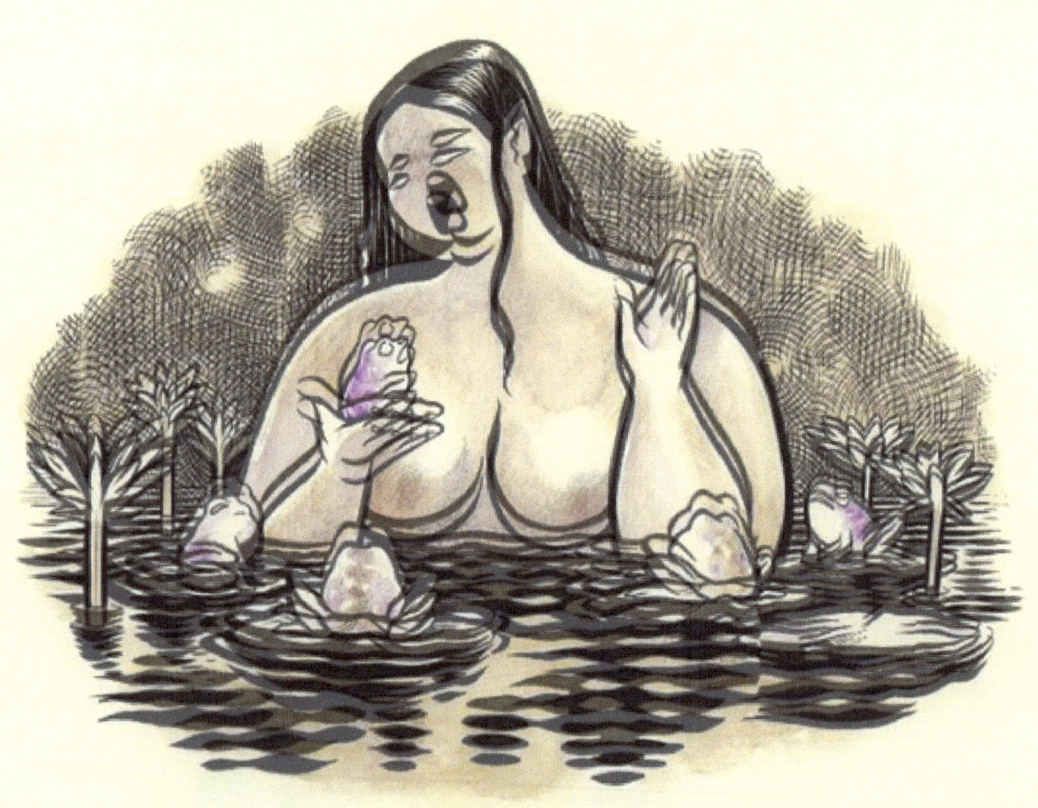

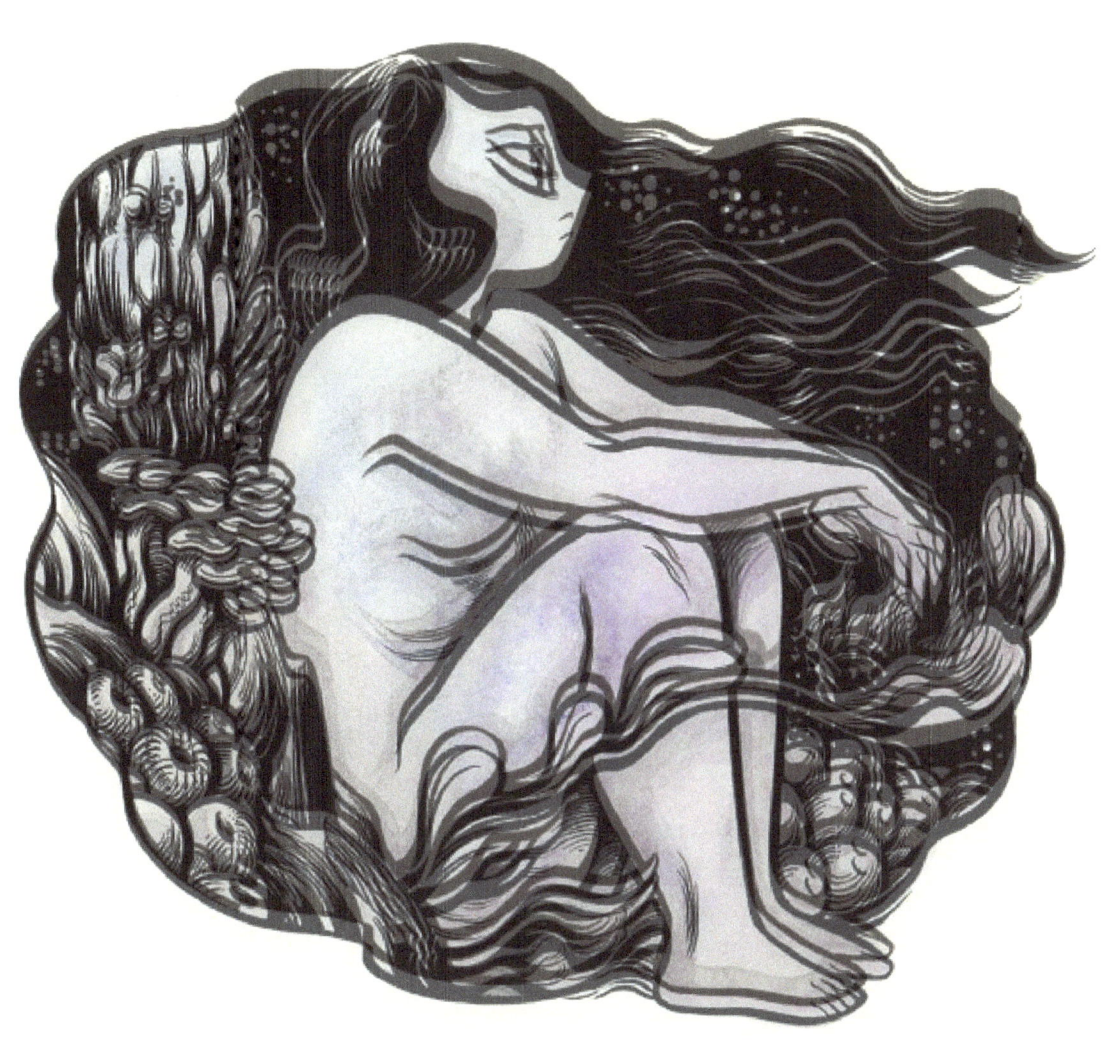

My head is so full
The thoughts are waterfalling
From my eyes
Filling up rivers
Streams of consciousness
And yet
My heart is so empty
A hollow organ that beats intermittently
Taking up space in my body
Vacancy available

How can I feel so full and empty
At the same time?

Fathom

It is easier to weep.
It is easier to grieve an ideation
than to spend your days hateful and hopeful,
chewing stubs from fingernails,
holding your breath until your lungs tear at their own veins,
waiting for something that was never yours to wait for.

I may not be capable of indifference,
but I am capable of such glorious renditions of longing.

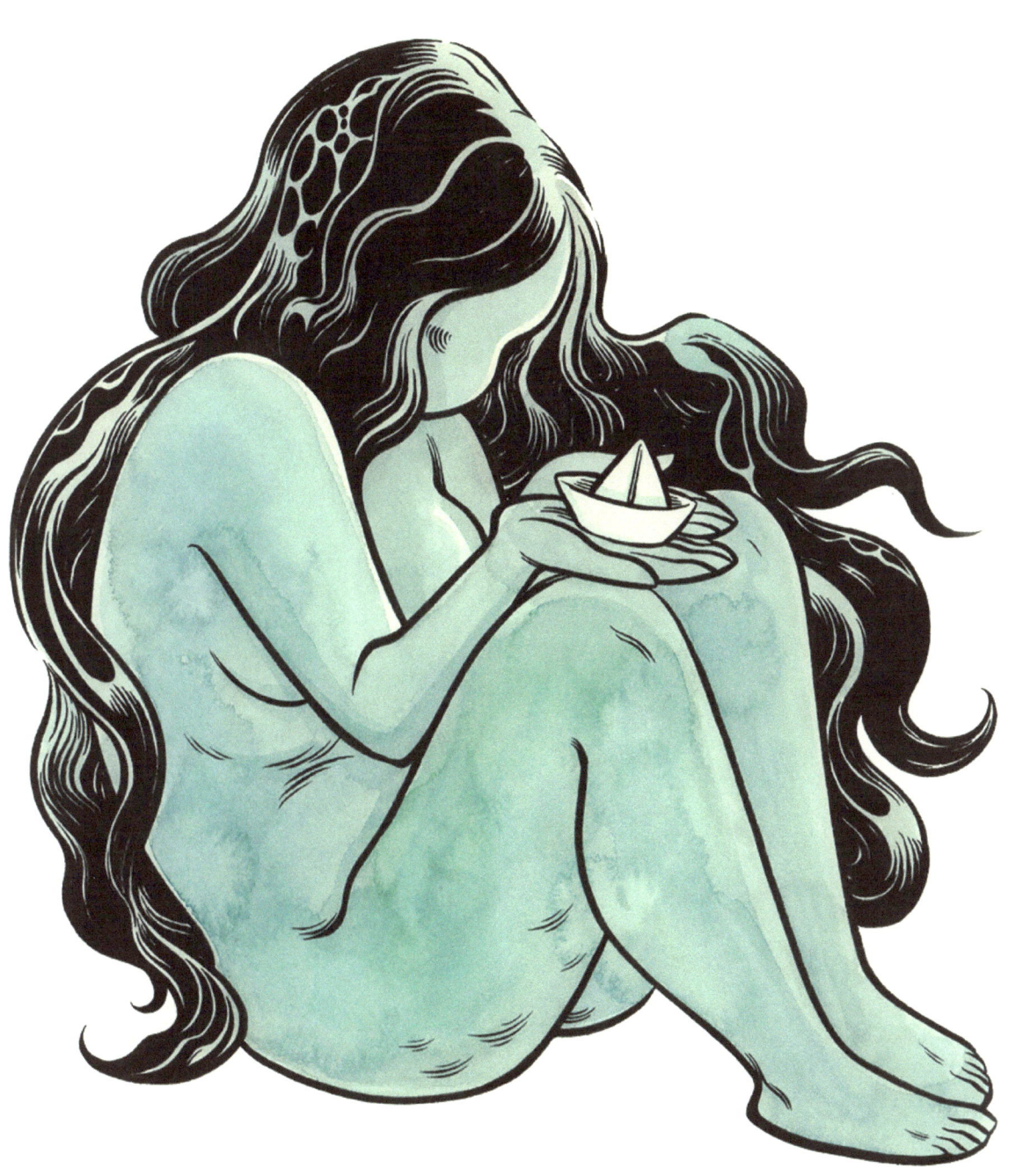

Nature summons me
Mothering me
I can feel her
Beneath me
My fingers inside of her
Deepest secrets
The dirt under my nails
From clawing my way out
Of this world
Into the depths of hers

How many times
Do I need to touch grass
In order to feel
Whole again?

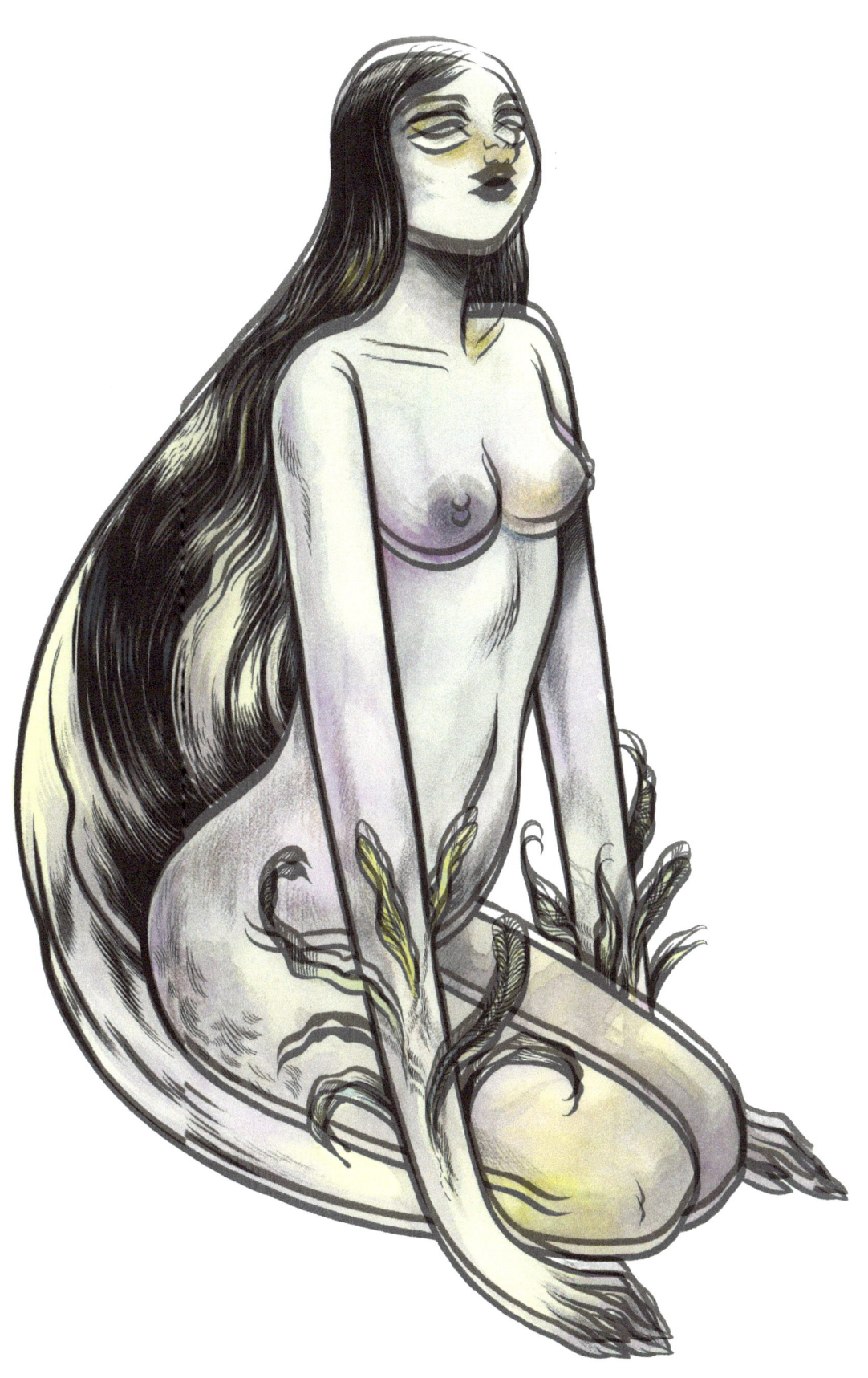

Demi-Gods

Us, who breathed magic
into mountains we dare not climb

and whispered life
into an oblivion we dare not face

Us, who begged skies and seas for moments;
mistaking its life for sentience

and worshipped ourselves at altars;
walking blind between our own pews

What are we if not gods?
What are the gods if not us?

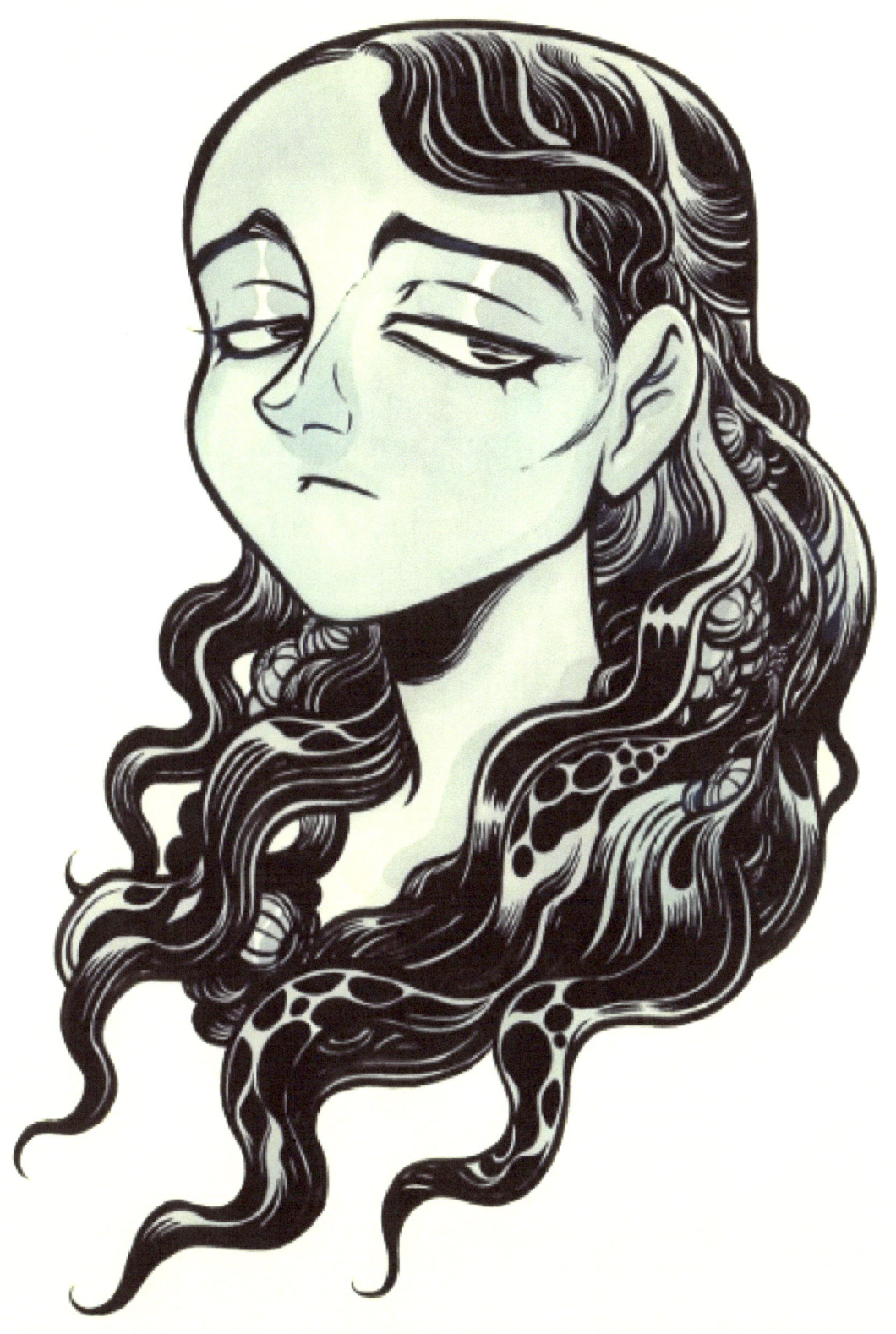

Bodies of Water

Take up space, please
Laugh like the fog rolling in
Scream like the waterfall at twilight
Embrace me like an ocean wave

We waste so much time and talent
paring ourselves down
Chipping away at the ancient grit of our skin
Casting off the thousand generations
of loved ones that manifest in our irises

Look at you — behaving as though
the stretch marks adorning your thighs
don't look like sunlight rippling on water,
as if the soul itself must be slim,
its crevices lined in water lilies

But you are not made of stone, my love,
you are not some pond fountain statue
ornamenting the landscape

You are made of sea and cicadas
Leaking dreams and kindness and pain
through the uneven notches of your teeth
A whole ecosystem thrives in your mind

The preservation of your tongue
is as worthy a cause as any

Hannah Jenkins

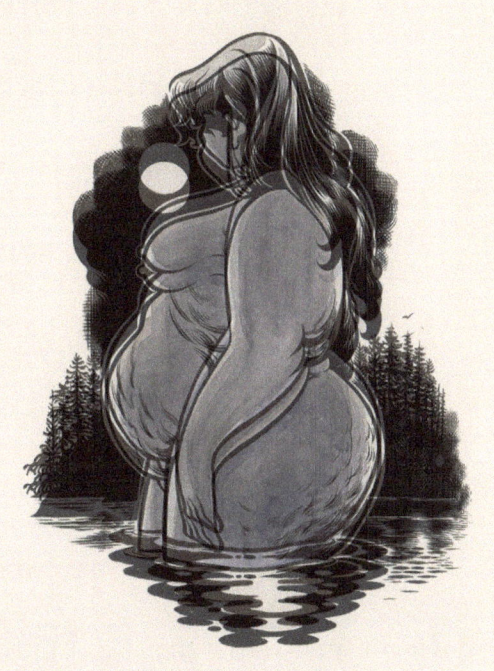

Beyond the Sea

I nodded to Ariel as I passed her emerging from the sea on her shaky new legs.

I offered her a sad smile,

knowing how different our journeys would be.

I laughed loudly as I stepped into the water,

then felt guilty, knowing she could not do the same.

Well, I thought, *she made her choice.*

And I had made mine.

I didn't have to trade my voice to a so-called "sea witch" to get what I wanted.

I had found a real one on land and simply told her what I desired.

I just want to be free, I said.

Because she was a real witch, I didn't have to explain myself,

nor did she ask for any part of me in return.

You've given enough, she smiled.

You must go to the sea.

On the beach, as Ariel searched for clothing to cover her new body,

I shed mine.

The water didn't ask for my modesty,

just as a real witch would never ask for a woman's voice.

It didn't hurt when my legs melted together, and scales began to grow.

In fact, I had never felt so free.

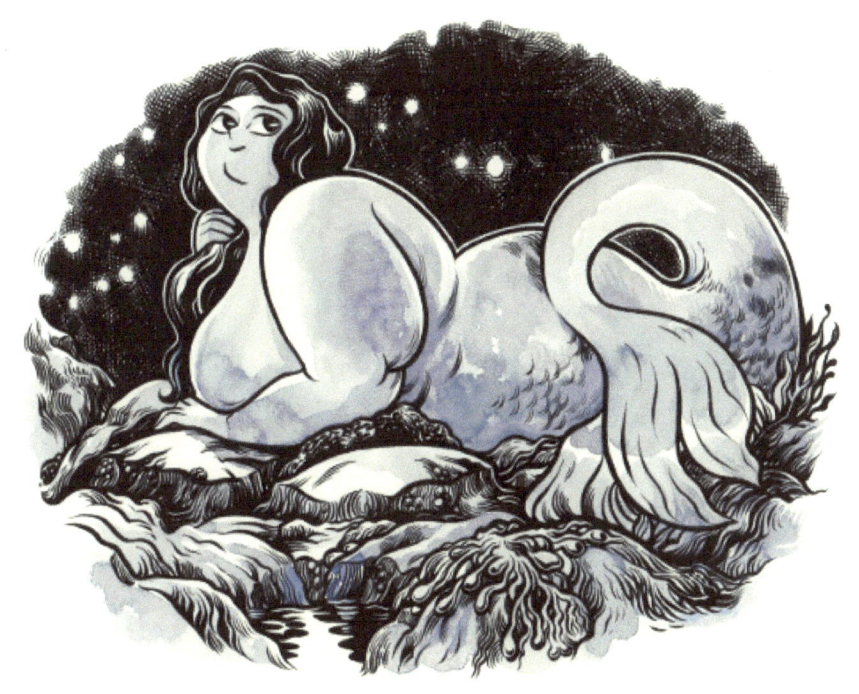

I sat on the bathroom counter,
Your blue eyes looking up at me
From the floor
How did I get here
With you?
I am young and I am new
To this side of the sexual sea

Your lips on mine
I run my hand over your head
Along your jaw
Down your neck and noticed
How your bra held your breasts
And I just wanted my hands to support you

Samm Joyy

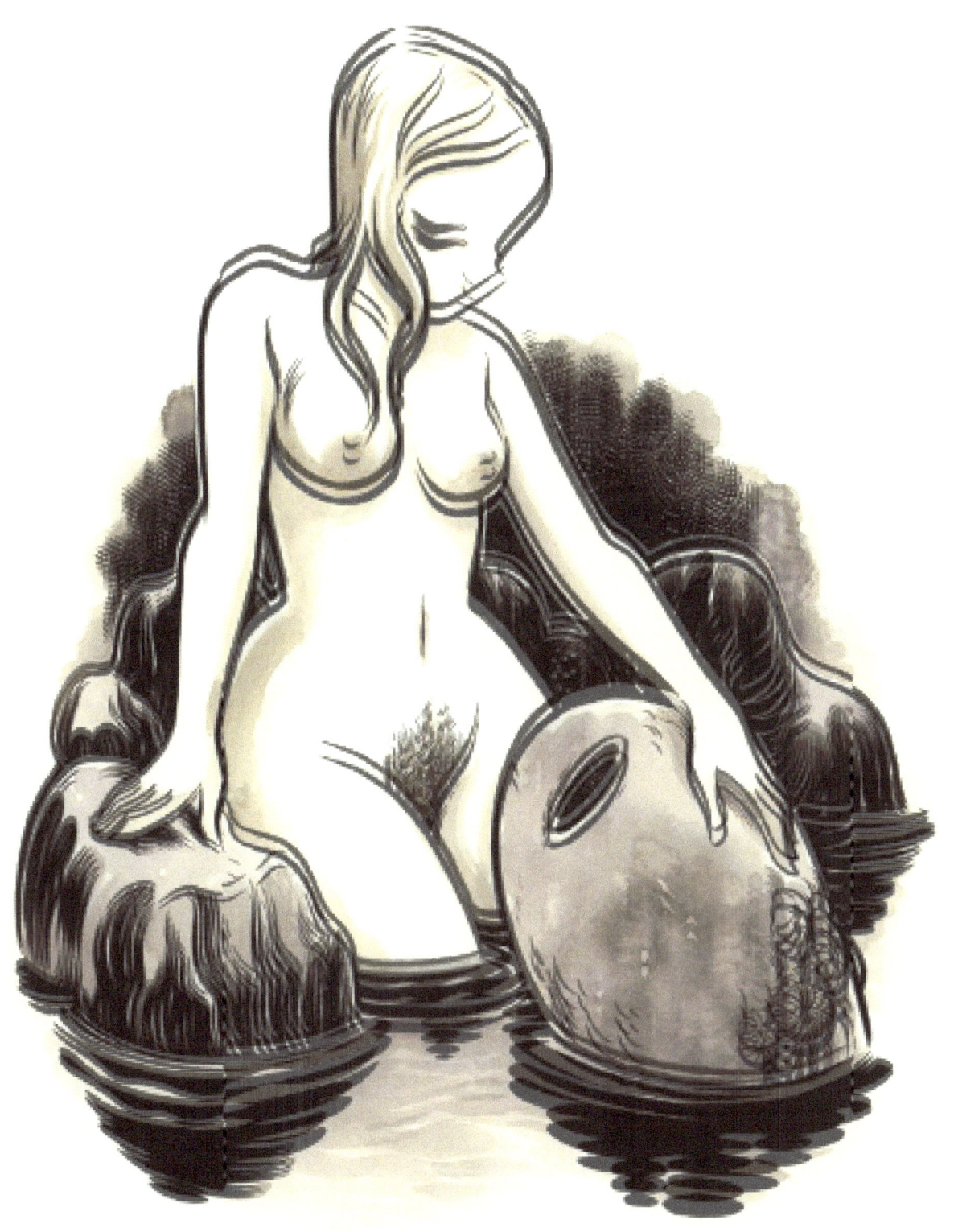

Cathedrals in Atlantis

Seaweed slick and bruised hip blue,
a tempered glass reflection,
an eye catch over sea salt shots
of holy water and communion wine

This metamorphosis of salvation —
the body dissolving like thin wet cardboard
on your tongue, promising you'll be made anew
once the calories settle into your bones

A confessional shade of gold, a periwinkle pew,
the windows bright with tomorrows,
a film of red forgiveness resting on the furniture like dust

That milky cascade of colour
shines upon the faces of God,
streaming sunlit through the stained glass,
casting something akin to a glint over my knees
like an evening orange caught in a wayward wave

I disturb the peace of the stoup,
a blessing dripping over breasts
and unwanted lungs

In the ripples of the basin,
I can see myself breathing

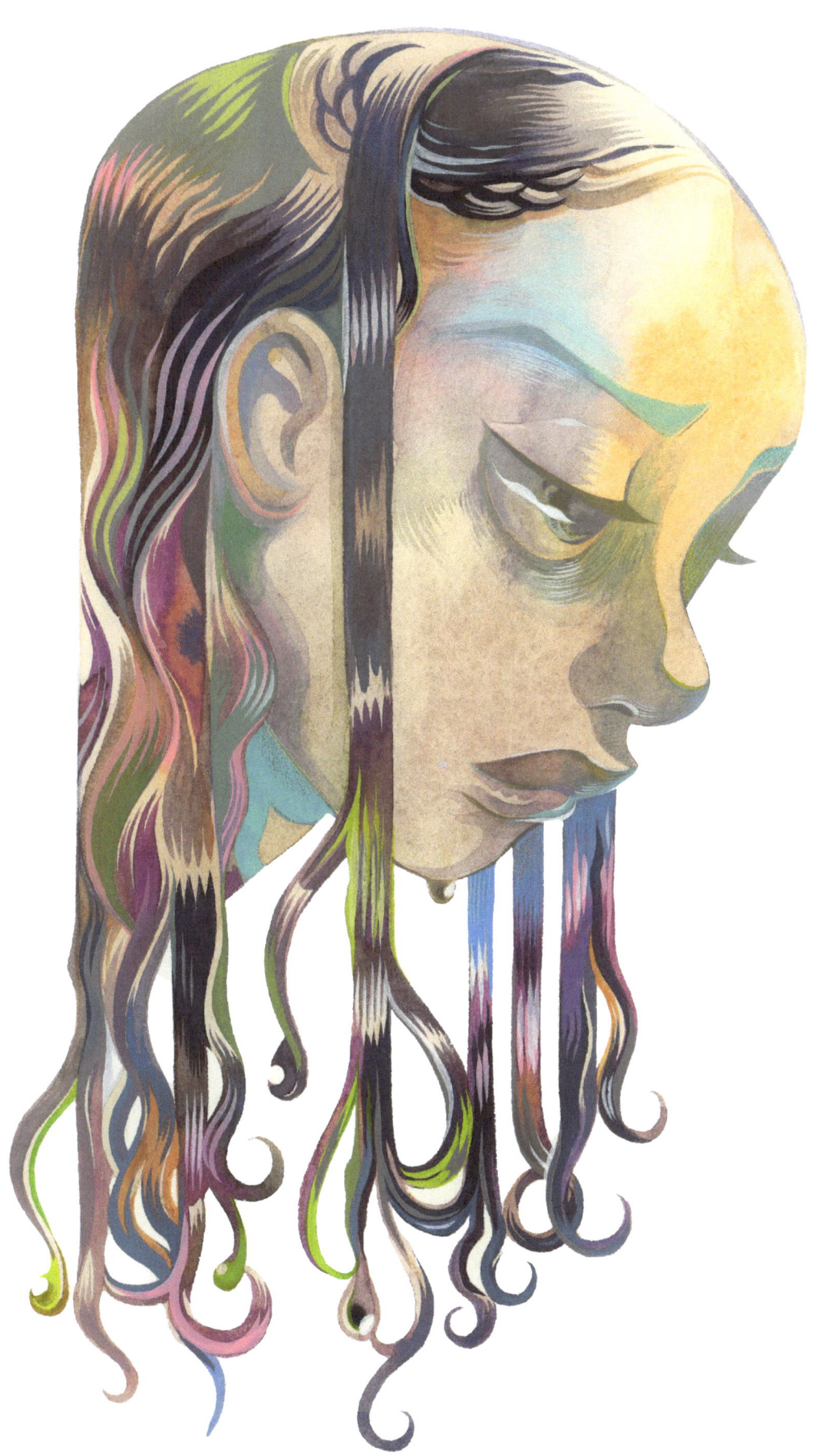

The Girl Who Never Stopped Bleeding

I was always afraid of the water.

When I was five, I was kicked out of swimming lessons for being hysterical and gripping my instructor's hair with my two tiny fists.

I don't remember what my swim instructor looked like, but I'll never forget the clumps of his reddish-brown hair that my mother wiped out of my palms after my last lesson.

The water was a stranger to me.

It was unknown and dangerous.

Like any good child of the 90s, my brain shouted *STRANGER DANGER* over and over any time I dipped my toes into any body of water I could not safely stand in.

I never understood why my mother was so frustrated with my failure to swim.

Every day, she put the fear of God into me over everything from drugs to dogs to deep fryers.

Everything else was out to kill me, so why couldn't she understand that the swimming pool was, too?

I never felt like I was missing out on anything special.

In fact, the water never even appealed to me until I started bleeding.

The day the blood first came, I cried, thinking I couldn't take a bubble bath that night.

My mother laughed at my ignorance,

You can still get a bath. The water stops the blood from coming out.

The idea seemed too good to be true.

I was gushing large, brown, gooey masses of blood.

Enough to fill a bathtub, I was sure.

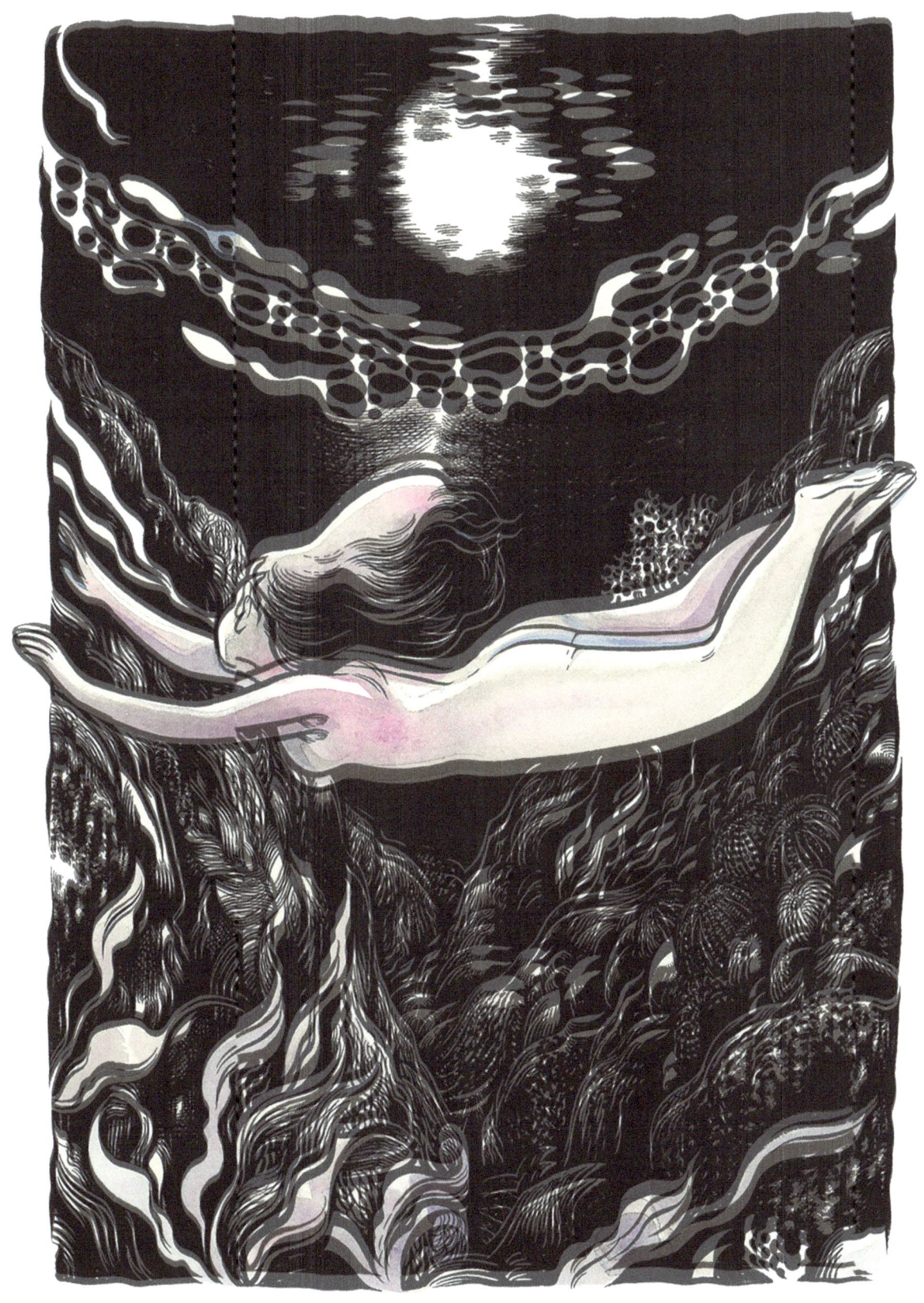

How could some mere water stop it?

I was shocked to learn my mother was not, in fact, a bold-faced liar.

The water, almost instantly, stopped the blood.

From then on, I'd spend my bloodiest days in the tub,

relieving myself from the mess.

What started as long baths on a few very specific days of the month,

turned into a solution for everything.

Scraped knee? Get in the water.

Nosebleed? Submerge self entirely.

Pop a pimple? Dive in headfirst.

My entire life became measured out in drops of blood.

More blood than my bathtub could possibly fix.

Enough blood to fill an ocean.

As I grew taller and wider,

and filled up with more blood,

I knew the water was no longer a stranger.

No longer a threat.

It was the only thing that could stop my eternal bleeding.

Only in the water could I be safe.

No stranger danger alarms went off as I submerged

myself that final time.

I felt the rocks beneath my feet drift away as I kicked off,

knowing that soon the blood would stop.

Krysta Fitzpatrick

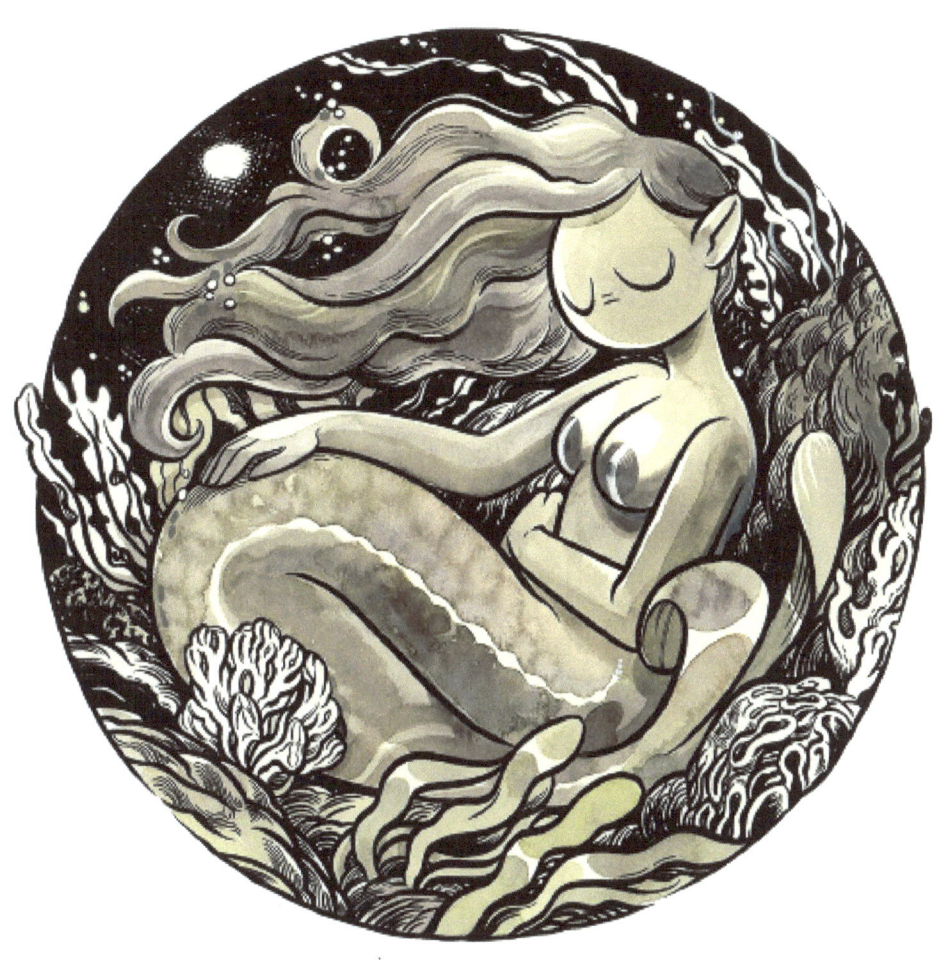

We're all trying
No one wants to give up
Or give in

But it's constantly there
The ache
I feel it in the depths
Of my stomach
In my bones
I'm trying to be invulnerable

I thank this body
For all the work it does
To keep me living

I cradle it gently
But tightly
Appreciating the support
It continues to offer
I thank this body
For without it, I would be just a spirit

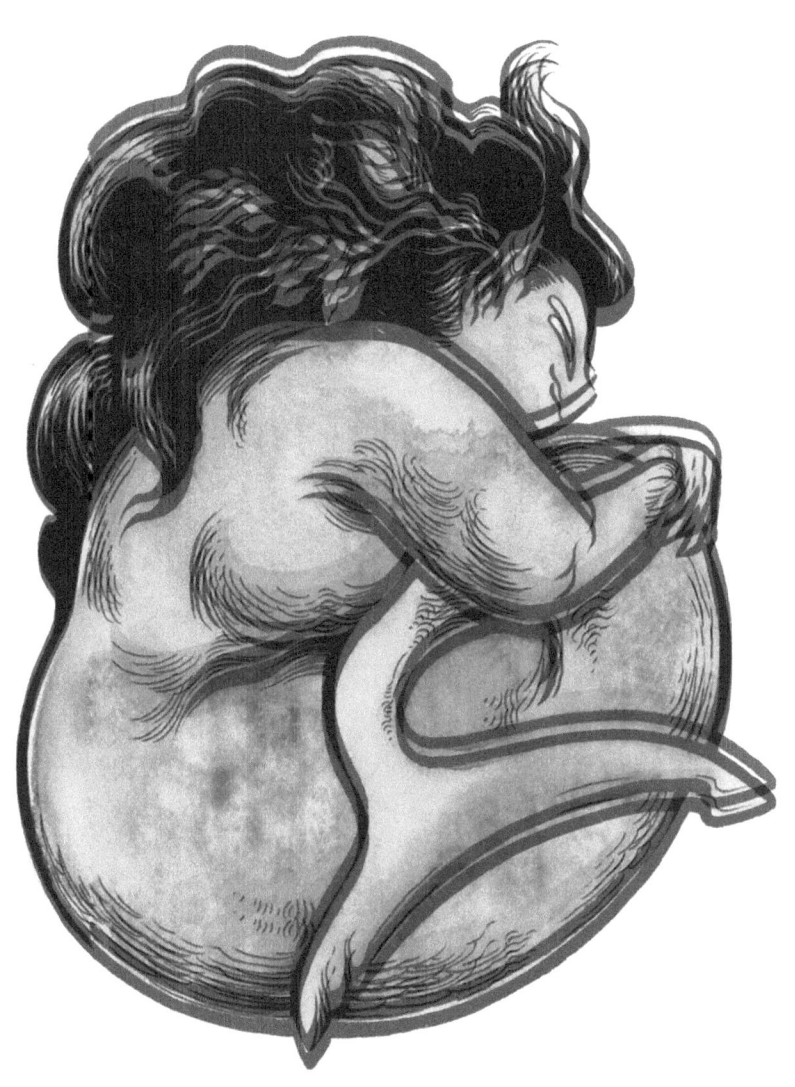

Black Moon Lilith

No one ever thinks about the first wives.

The women who came before June Carter or Ava Gardner.

The women who held them down at their worst and were abandoned at their best.

Not that there was ever any "holding down" permitted in my marriage,

no matter how hard he tried.

I've spent centuries in the shadow of Eve.

Eve this. Eve that. Eve: The First Woman.

Except...she wasn't.

I stood on the Earth from which I was formed long before Eve was dreamt out of some man's rib.

I came from no man and would allow no man to come from me.

I would not lie below.

No snake had to trick me into disobeying my "father",

I whispered to them willingly while my husband slept, dreaming of a wife who would bear him sons and laugh at his jokes.

I smiled with snakes and plotted my escape long before Eve was ever cast out.

People often forget that.

I don't hate Eve, though. Far from it.

Sure, my name continues to fade from the memories of the masses,

but at least I have not been made the eternal scapegoat.

The woman responsible for "the fall of man."

(Although I would like to point out that putting one of the world's most delicious and aesthetically pleasing fruits on a tree and then telling two people with the mental capacity of toddlers that they weren't allowed to eat them was the ultimate cruel power move. The woman was set up for failure!)

Let them draw me naked, draped in my snakes,

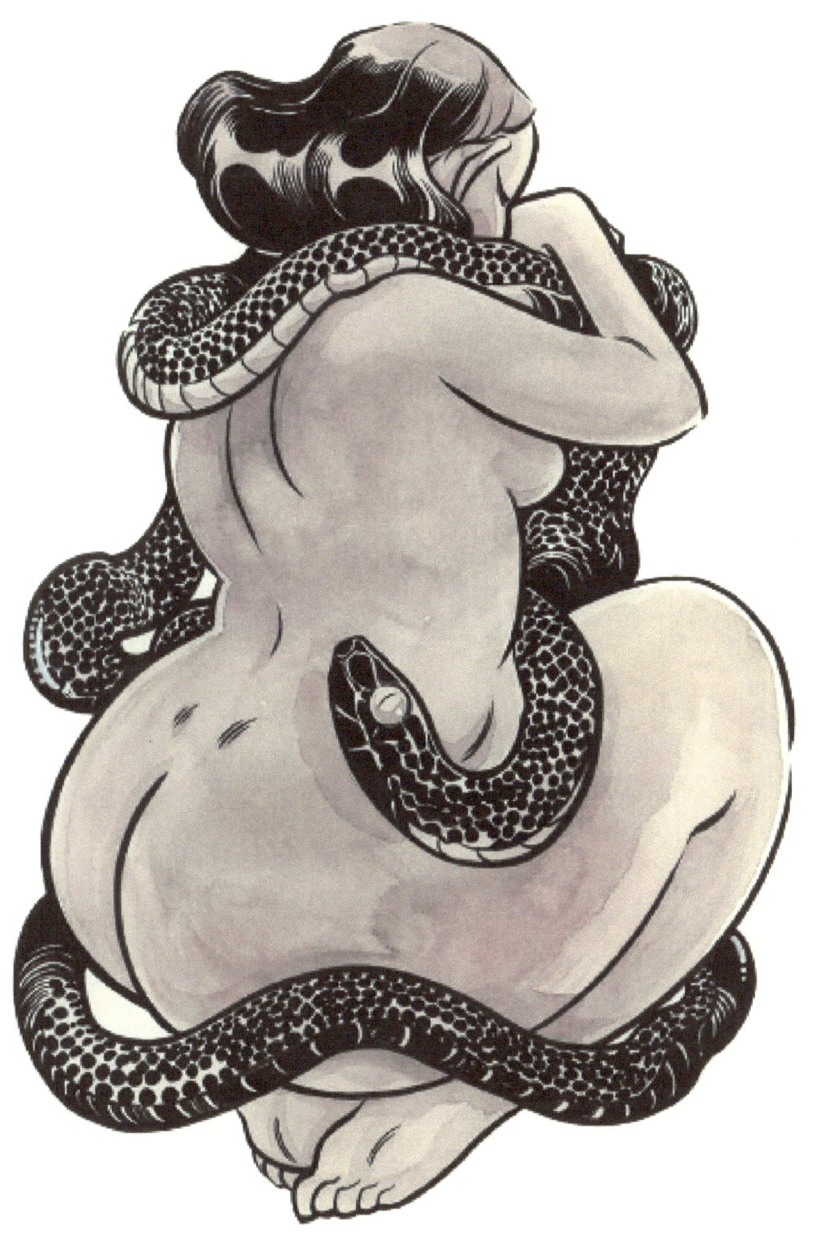

Krysta Fitzpatrick

then let them forget me.

I never wanted a garden, anyway.

Let poor Eve hold the responsibility for the bumps in your husbands' throats,

but know that I left so no husband could ever hold his hand to mine.

Pickings

I have formed a nasty habit of picking at the skin between my thighs. Along the cavern between my knees, there is now a sandy floor of bloated red masses and coarse hairs stuck under agitated follicles.

My favourite is when it spews out an infected seafoam green. By noon the denim of my jeans will have rubbed the open sore into a large mountainous cyst. I know the anger lingers below the surface, that I've done nothing but make it scream. But the picking continues, invasive.

More than once, the thought of gluing my thighs shut has pierced through. Of simply eliminating the area I have ruined so irrevocably. I imagine a bulky tail spurting below my navel, scaled and slippery like a fish.

I sometimes think of removing my skin entirely, pulling it back with a potato peeler and starting over. Grow new fresh stuff that feels easy to touch and even easier to lose hold of. A raw freak of nature evading hands and flopping her way back to the water. Back to my coral reef of a cubicle and the school of minnows being let out for the day and the shipwreck with its broken bottles weathered to pebbles where the bones of my knees lie hidden beneath the planks.

Hannah Jenkins

Krysta Fitzpatrick

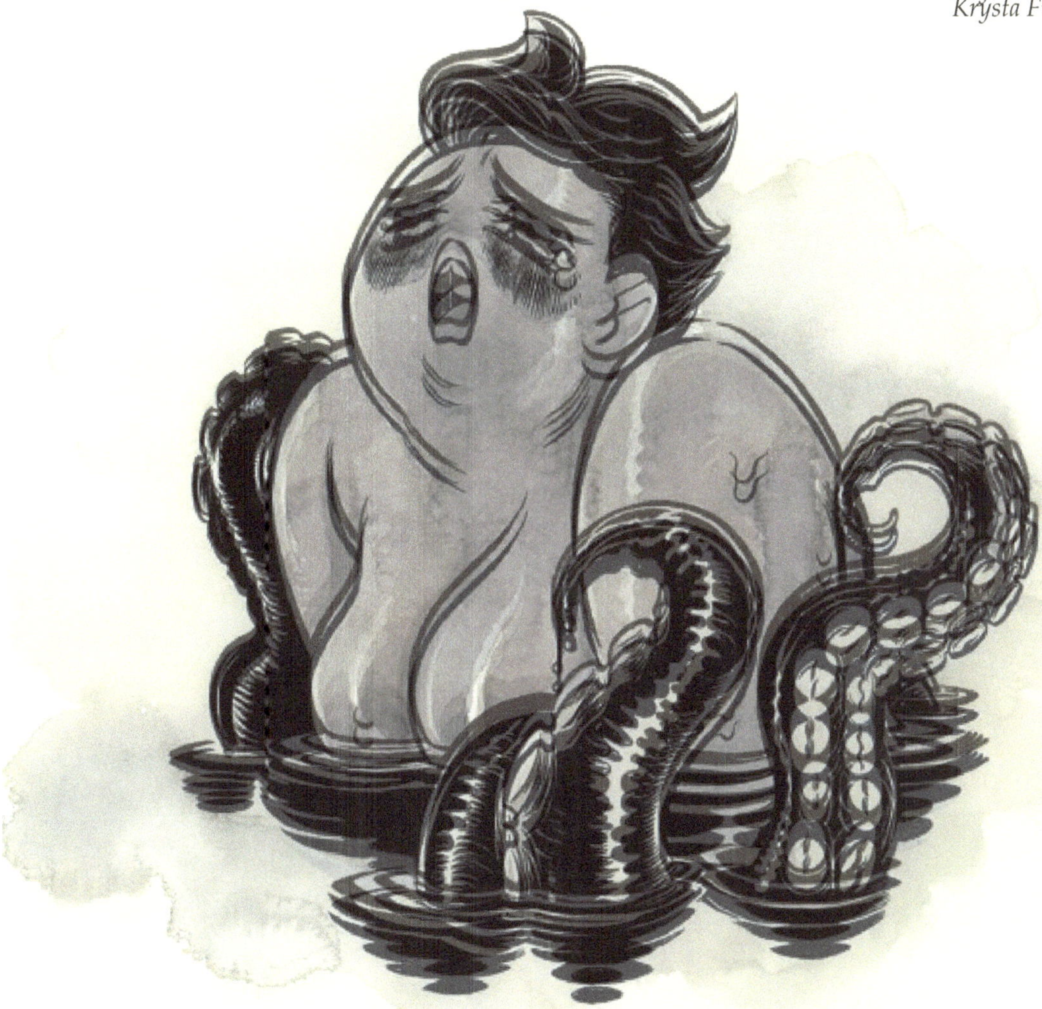

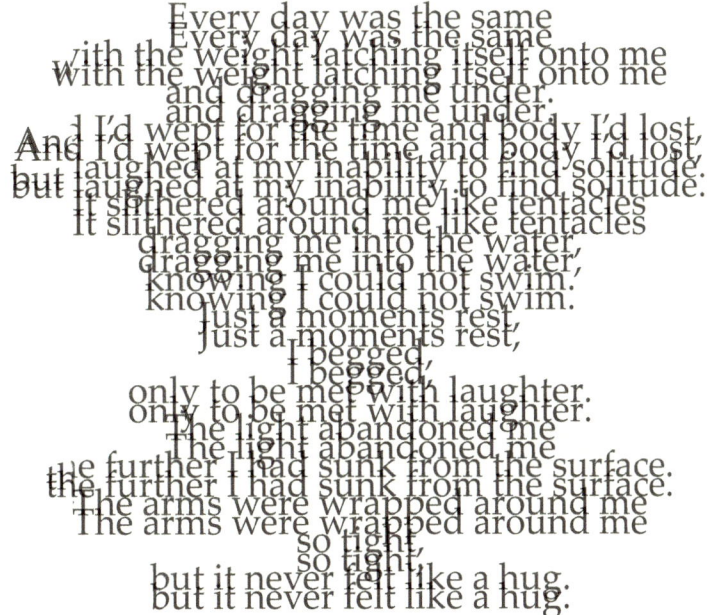

Honestly and Deeply

Every day was the same
with the weight latching itself onto me
and dragging me under.
And I'd wept for the time and body I'd lost,
but laughed at my inability to find solitude.
It slithered around me like tentacles
dragging me into the water,
knowing I could not swim.
Just a moments rest,
I begged,
only to be met with laughter.
The light abandoned me
the further I had sunk from the surface.
The arms were wrapped around me
so tight,
but it never felt like a hug.

Everything Nice

Sugar and spice,
and everything nice.
That's what little girls are made of.
I wrote and re-wrote this poem so many times,
but I always started with that.
Sugar and spice and everything nice.
Is that what little girls are made of?

I was 8 years old the first time a boy my own age told me I was sexy.
He got me a popsicle from his father's freezer,
and I ate it on my grandmother's veranda.

I was eleven the first time a grown man stared at me for too long
in a way that filled my insides up with rocks, which he would
surely use to weigh my body down when he wanted to get rid of
the evidence.

Maybe I'm made of popsicle sticks and beach rocks?

By the time I was eleven, I knew I had to be afraid all the time,
though what I was meant to be afraid of wasn't always so clear.

Eleven is a big age for a girl.
You're all sugar and spice and everything nice, and then
BOOM!
You're a creature emerging naked from a lagoon,
feral and wild.
Small breasted and childlike,
blood running down your legs.
Terrified and terrifying all at once.

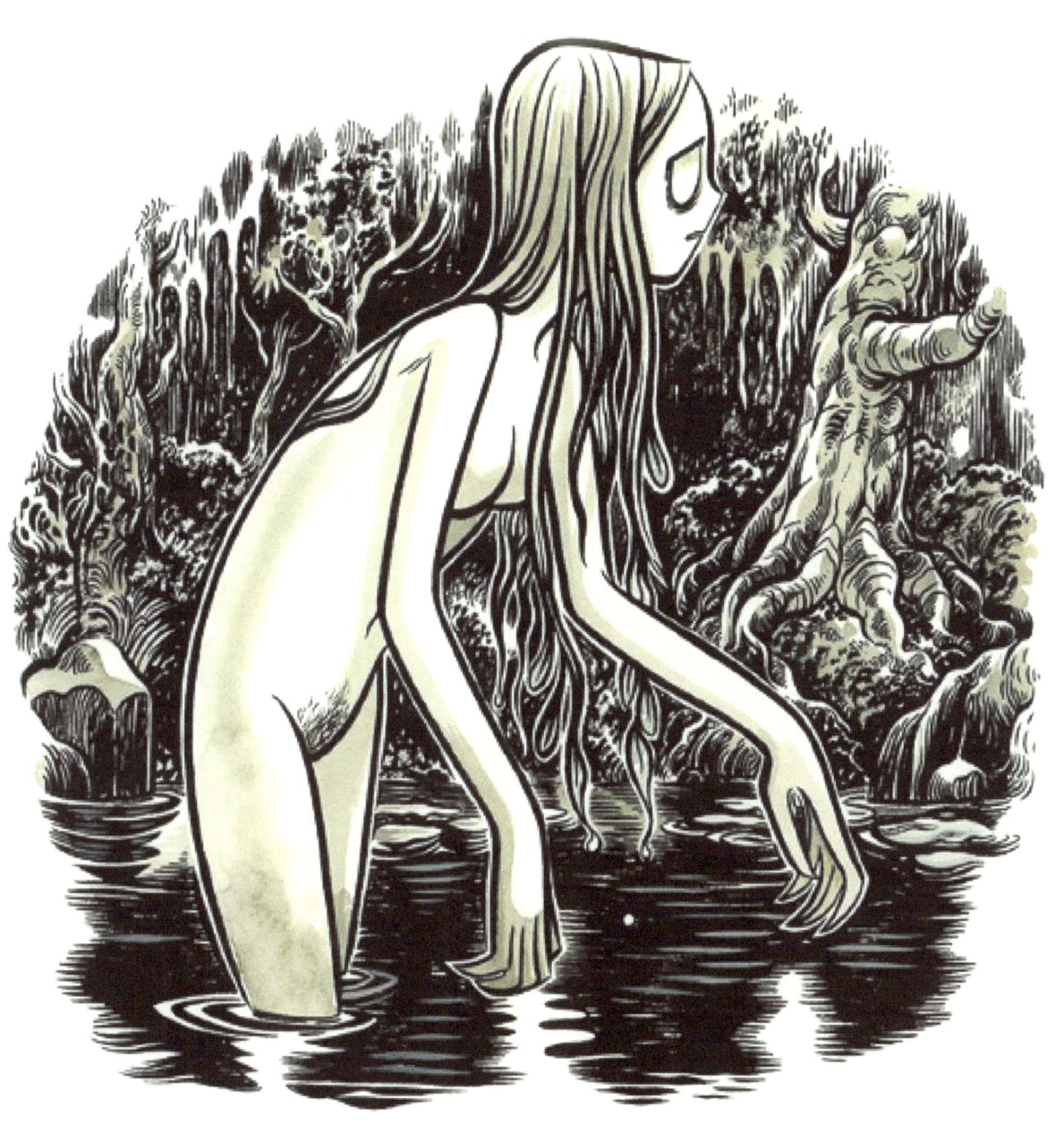

Suddenly girlhood isn't made up of everything nice.
It stops being five cent candies and rub on tattoos.
Instead, it becomes being told to go put some clothes on
because there are men in this house,
even when those men are your own flesh and blood.

Girlhood becomes being told to stay away from boys
because they only want one thing,
but for the love of God be nice to the boys,
you don't want to seem like a bitch.

Girlhood is being told to use your tiny fingers like talons so their
DNA will be found under your nails. Your body is weak, but it's
also a weapon.

Girlhood is asking politely, and then eventually begging, that
no one touch the green ribbon around your neck, but always
knowing some thoughtless man will eventually untie it, because
heaven forbid you have something that is entirely your own.

If I could pour out all my sugar and spice,
I would.
I'd rather be made of arsenic and crushed up peach pits.
That would really be nice.

Krysta Fitzpatrick

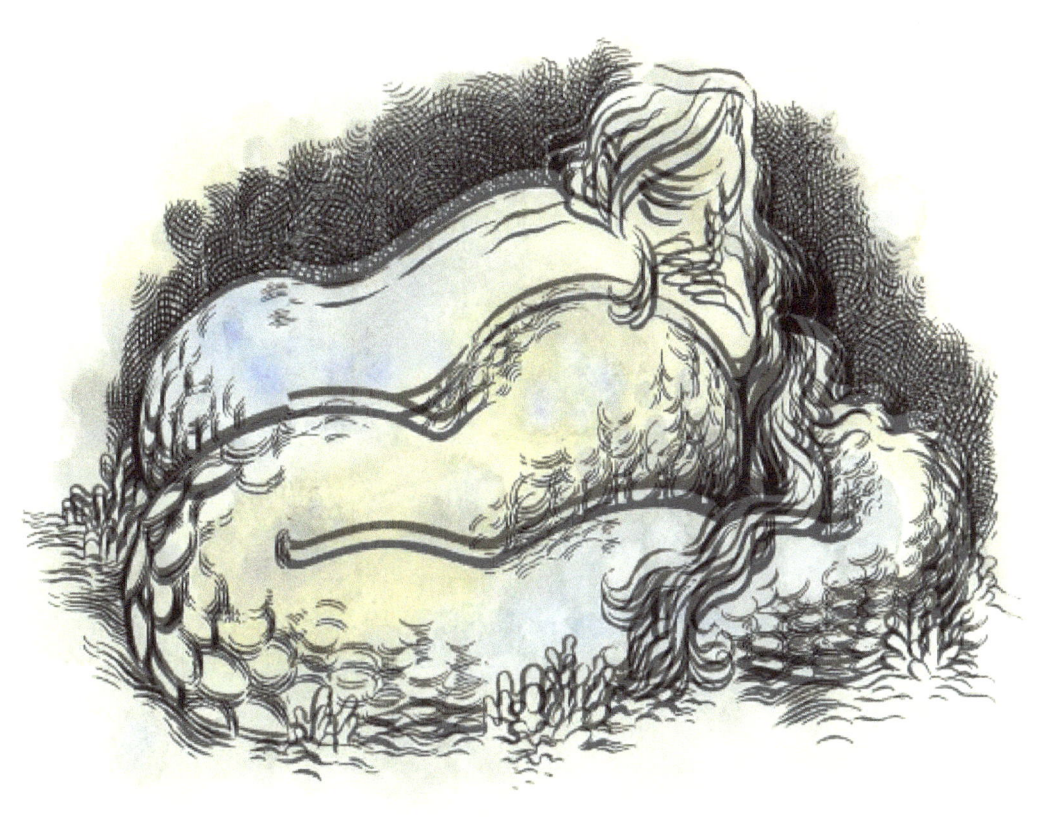

If I become visibly invisible
Maybe no one will see
How lonely you left me
I'd rather not be seen
A chameleon
Not to be perceived
If I become visibly invisible
Maybe no one will notice
My lack of desire
The spark in my eyes
Can no longer set a fire
To my will to live

Samm Joyy

It took some time
But I can feel it
– Change –
I grew my hair out long
Something to hide behind

And with one hand
You brushed it back
And found me -bare-

It took some time
But I can feel it
– Changing –
I am changing

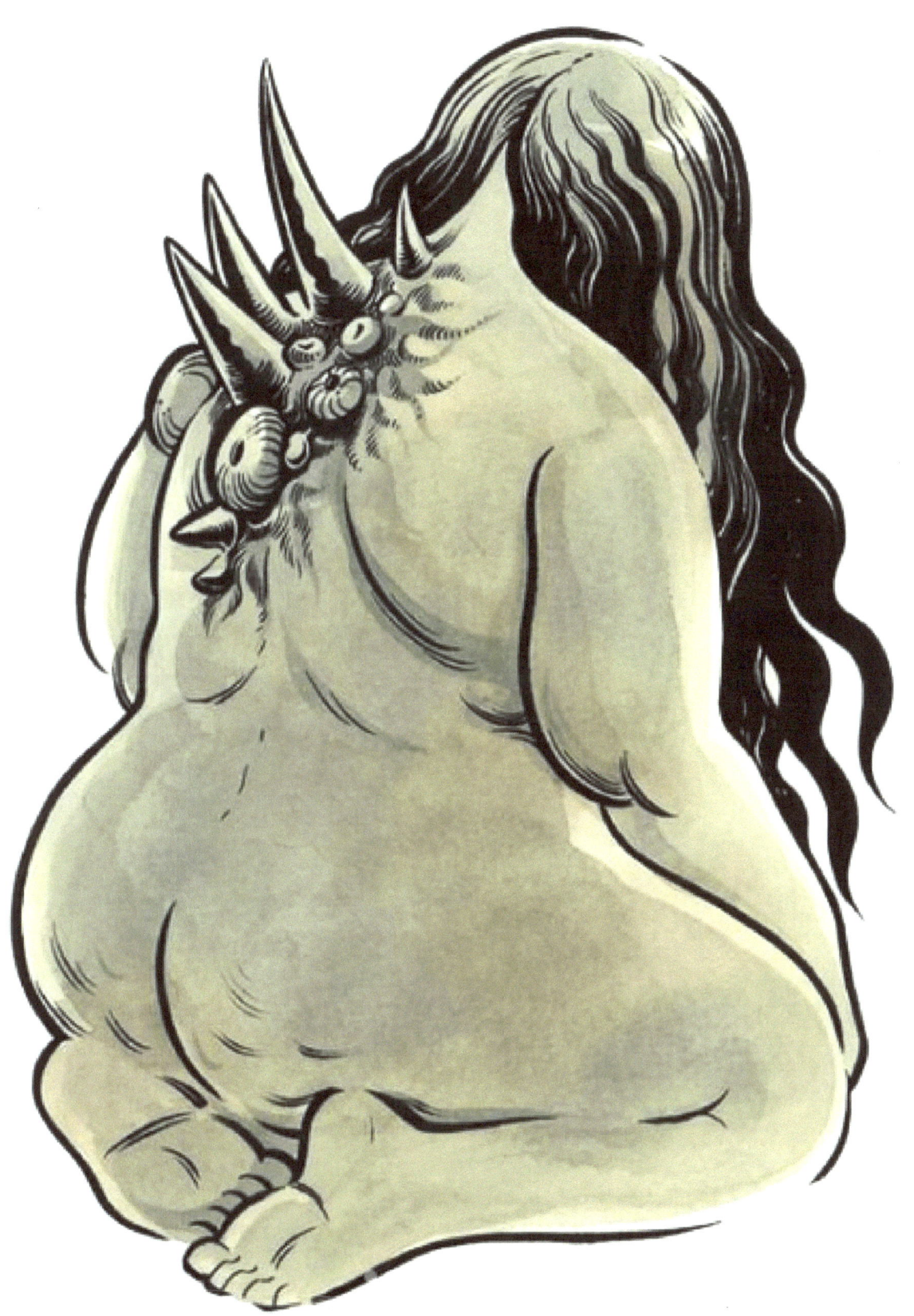

Girl's Girl
For Gisèle Pelicot, the ultimate girl's girl:

For those of us who had grown feral,
and had to claw our way out of the graves we did not dig,
only to find we were too tired to speak when the air hit our faces:

For those of us who turned into shadows of our former selves,
fading into the background
of the lives we thought we knew so well:

For those of us who were pushed back through gates
that had been kept closed by other women
who thought we were less than them:

For those of us who believed in the war on men,
never realizing it was always an attack on femininity,
because who would ever want to be like us?

For those of us who sat in our shame,
and let it turn us into things we could not recognize
no matter how much that shame did not belong to us:

We thank you.
For naming names,
even when those names were so close to home.

We thank you.
For showing your face,
even if it didn't look like the picture-perfect image of a beautiful young victim.

We thank you:
For loudly and boldly using your voice
to remind us that the shame wasn't ours to hold;

We thank you:
For letting go of the only life you knew,
because a woman's body is a home, not a war zone.

We thank you:
For being a girl's girl,
and shedding light on the violence our bodies carry every fucking day;

We thank you.

Krysta Fitzpatrick

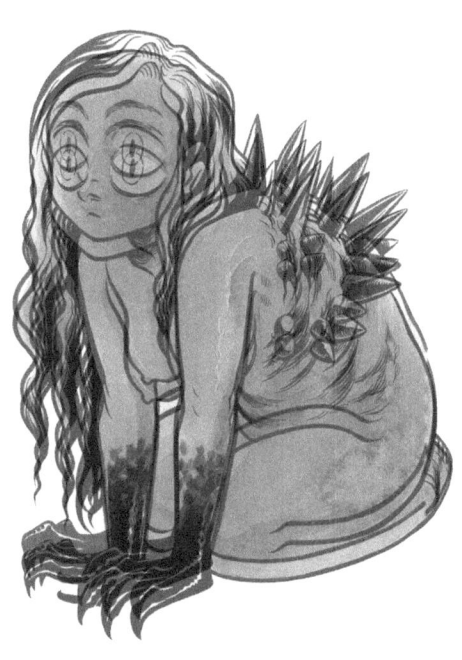

He called me an exhibitionist
As I undressed
The curtains open
I'd rather the world see my body
Than infiltrate my mind
If I can distract them long enough with desire
They won't notice the depression
That's been sprouting from my body
Expanding in my lungs
Until I burst

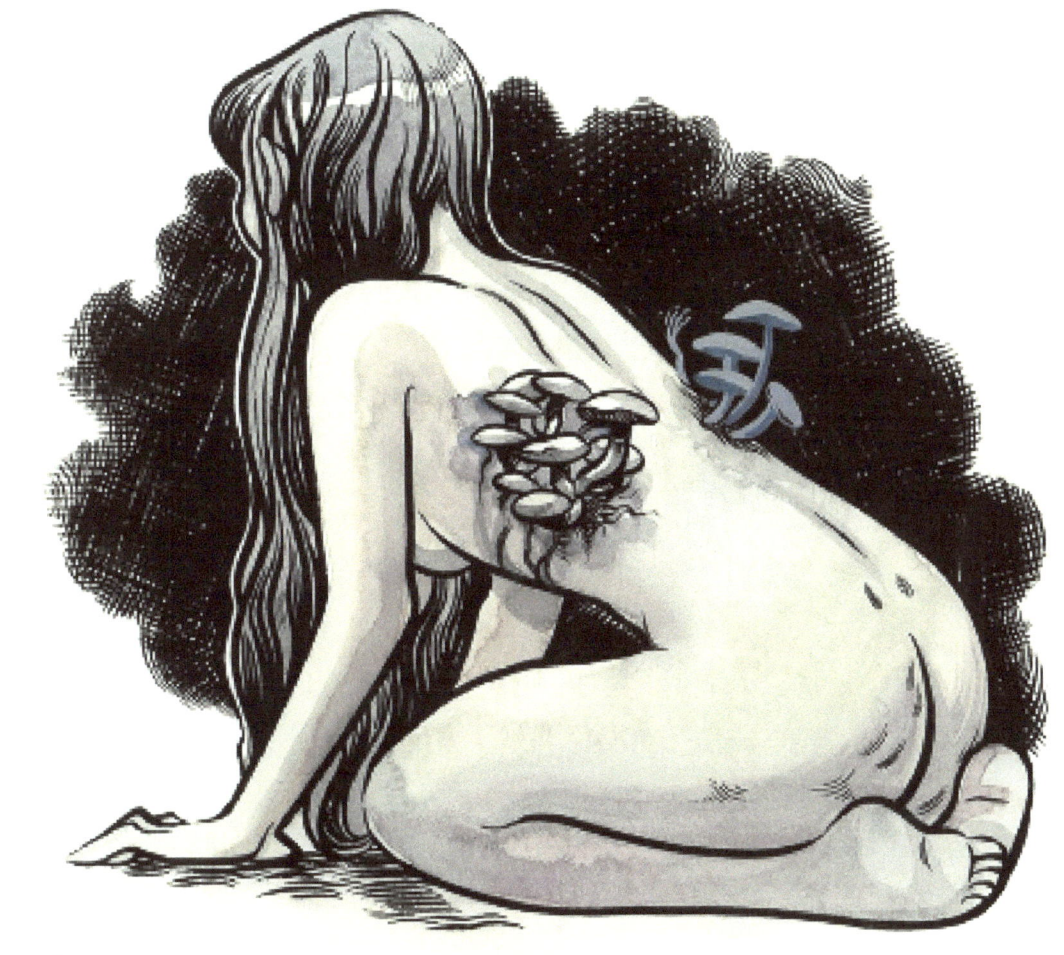

Samm Joyy

Seep

The unwanted collect like dust mites on my water logged hair

To scratch would be to tear the scalp from bone

To remove the remnants would be to remove skin

The stellerid fuses to me and
we share the same murky lifeforce =
a polluted concoction of oil and grime
and something that was once water

a seashell eats its way through my left ear
while sand slots into my pores like men to war

The evening tide echoes in

poseidon,   neptune,   triton

Fishermen chase schools as though
the tides were nothing but a place
and not a creature itself,   pulsating and   vast,
sharks like red blood cells with coral reef livers
and cyclone lungs

The wooden planks of shore sink lazily to my toes,
a torn mainsail hugs my shoulder like a skin graft
and the captain
catches in my hair,
bloated and putrid

There is no god in the ocean

There is only me

Hannah Jenkins

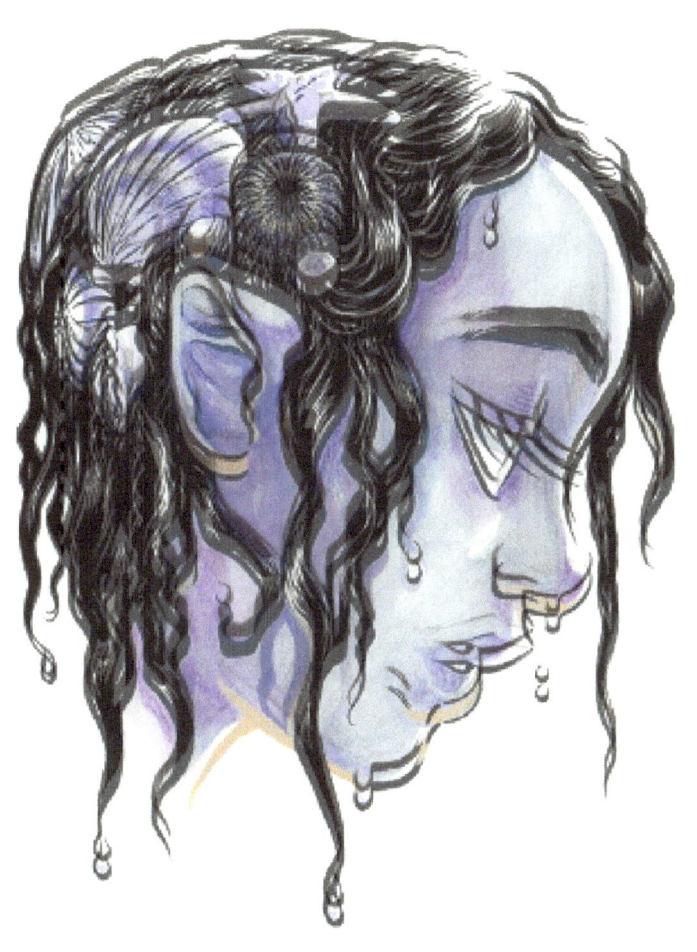

Le bal des folles

You terrify me, he said,
meaning it as an insult.
Good, I thought,
knowing how important it was that men feared me more
than they desired me.

They used to burn women like me,
call us witches and mystics,
but we'd just cackle as the flames ate us up.

They used to drown women like me,
tie us to boulders and throw us in a lake,
where we'd feast on eel guts and fisheyes.

They used to lock up women like me,
throw us in madhouses with padded cells,
where we'd make dresses out of bedsheets and throw
lavish balls.

You're crazy, they'd say
to the women who hungered without shame,
but then it was too late, as we'd be upon them.

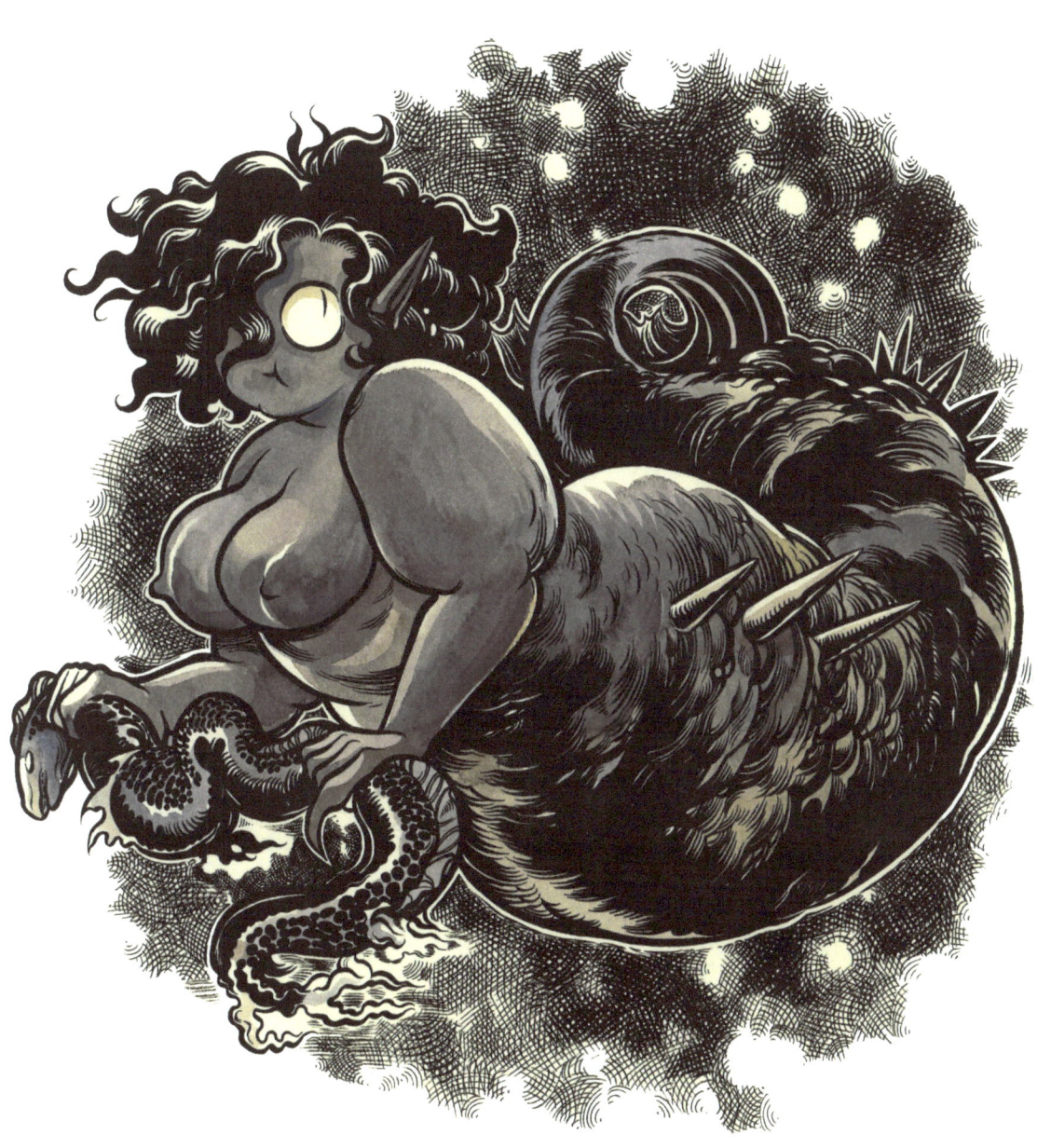

Sodden Women

Nana warned me of mad creatures like these
They're clammy and calloused and likely diseased
They live in the seas, marshes, lagoons
They crawl out of rivers with voices that croon

These heathens with hordes and anger and dirt
Scratching remains from the sea, wicked and curt
They'll scoop out your eyes to season their stew
Put your fingernails on saucers, claim it's your dues

So we learn quite young to never venture from shore
There are mad women out there, made out of scorn
Cooked up with greed by some malevolent god
Insatiable, poisonous, stalking the bog

But I yearn some nights to visit the water
If only to test these strange theories of slaughter
For I always envision something cozy, benign
Collectors, borrowers, of simple design

Do we not all love with a heat that is maddening?
Eyelids burning, our tears impassioning?
What crime was it that brought you to their door?
That they wanted something you had learned to deplore?

What a punishable offence, to stay where you are
To bite your intruders, to mangle, to mar
And how common for us to concoct into lore
The voiceless bodies that darken our morgue

Nana said the creatures would never see reason
They're mute, stubborn, iniquitous demons
But I wonder, sometimes, if they're as bad as we believe
and worry, deep down, that they're an awful lot like me

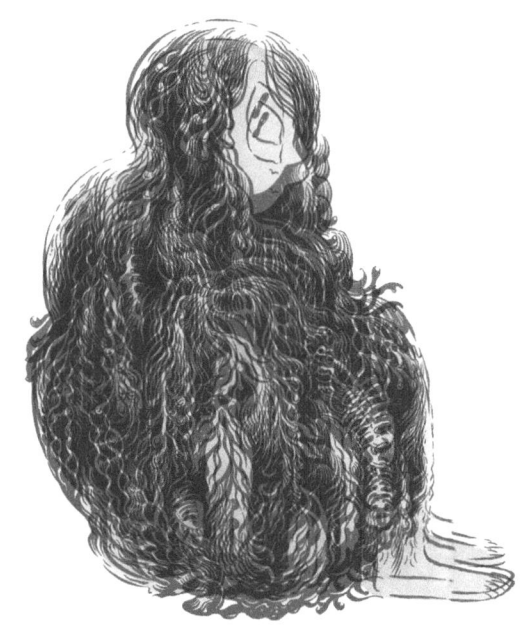

Hannah Jenkins

Old Wives' Tale

That's an old wives' tale, they say

about all the things they don't believe in.

A superstition, a folk story, an urban legend.

The old hag, the banshee, the wailing woman, the witch.

She made it up.

She isn't real.

Refuse profane and old wives' fables, and exercise thyself unto godliness,

it says in the King James Bible.

But what is the Bible, other than folk tales told by men?

Who defines godliness?

Husbands, fathers, sons, and brothers.

Are their stories true because they are written down?

Or is what separates a legend from the truth simply what lies between the storyteller's legs?

We build gold and marble churches for the stories of men,

but relegate the knowledge of women to back-room whispers.

Unverified, exaggerated, fabricated.

Who could possibly believe a story told by a woman?

For what could a woman possibly know that a man did not?

I can't help by laugh when someone asks me about my religious affiliations,

then proudly announce, my religion is *Old Wives' Tales.*

Krysta Fitzpatrick

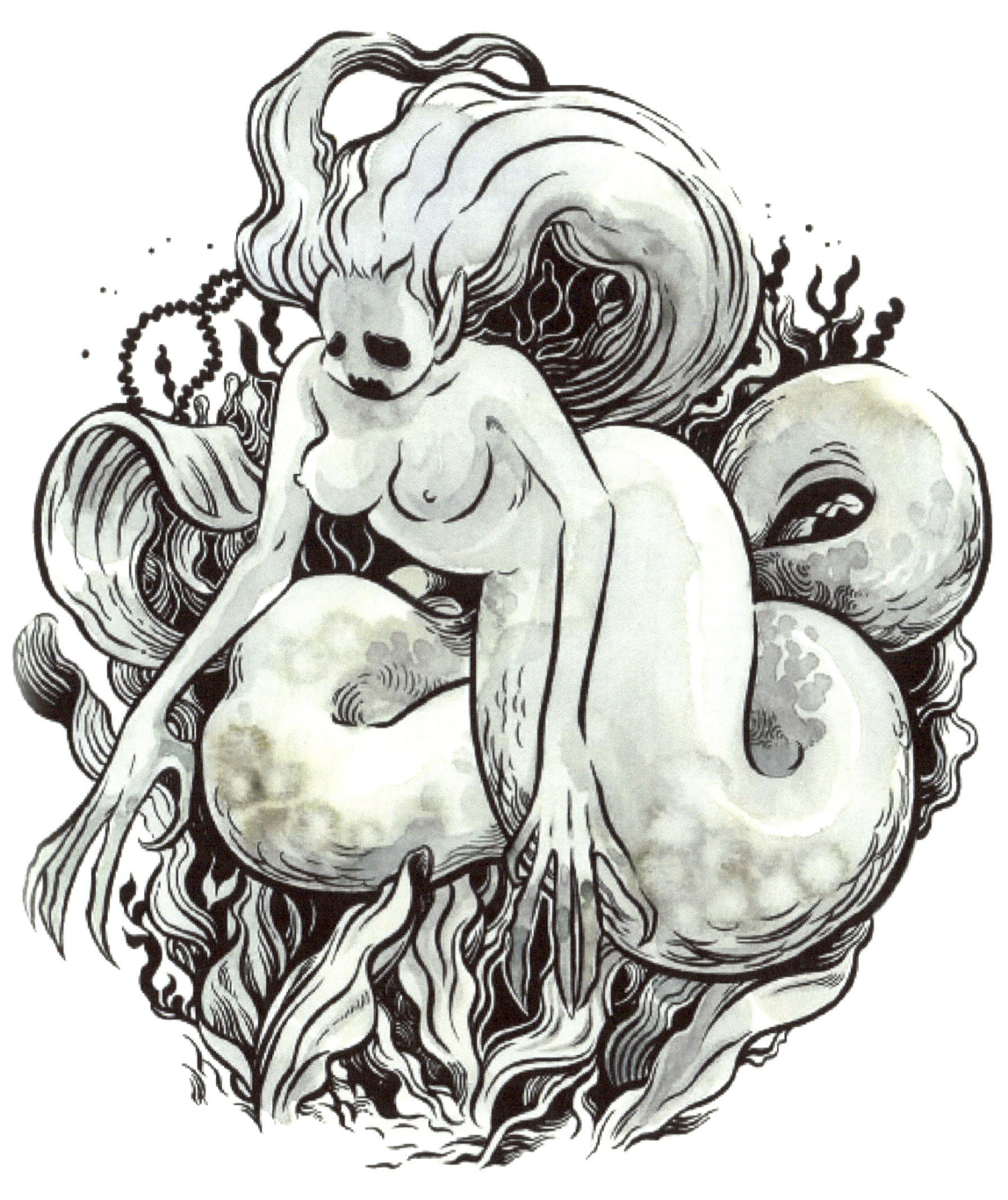

The Steeple of the Sea Witch

The still knotted end of a balloon rests
in the pincer sharp grasp of a crab,
a cigarette butt taints the pond trail
with flankers and grey-white ash,
a plastic Christmas tree ornament
sits tattered by the shoreline
shreds of polyethylene
still clinging to its hook

You breathe like you were owed it
Chain smoking on a pier, behaving
as though the mud beneath
your boots cannot shift
or the steady monster
of the stream cannot rise

Ignorant to the horrors
of the deep; unaware

I have driven men mad for less

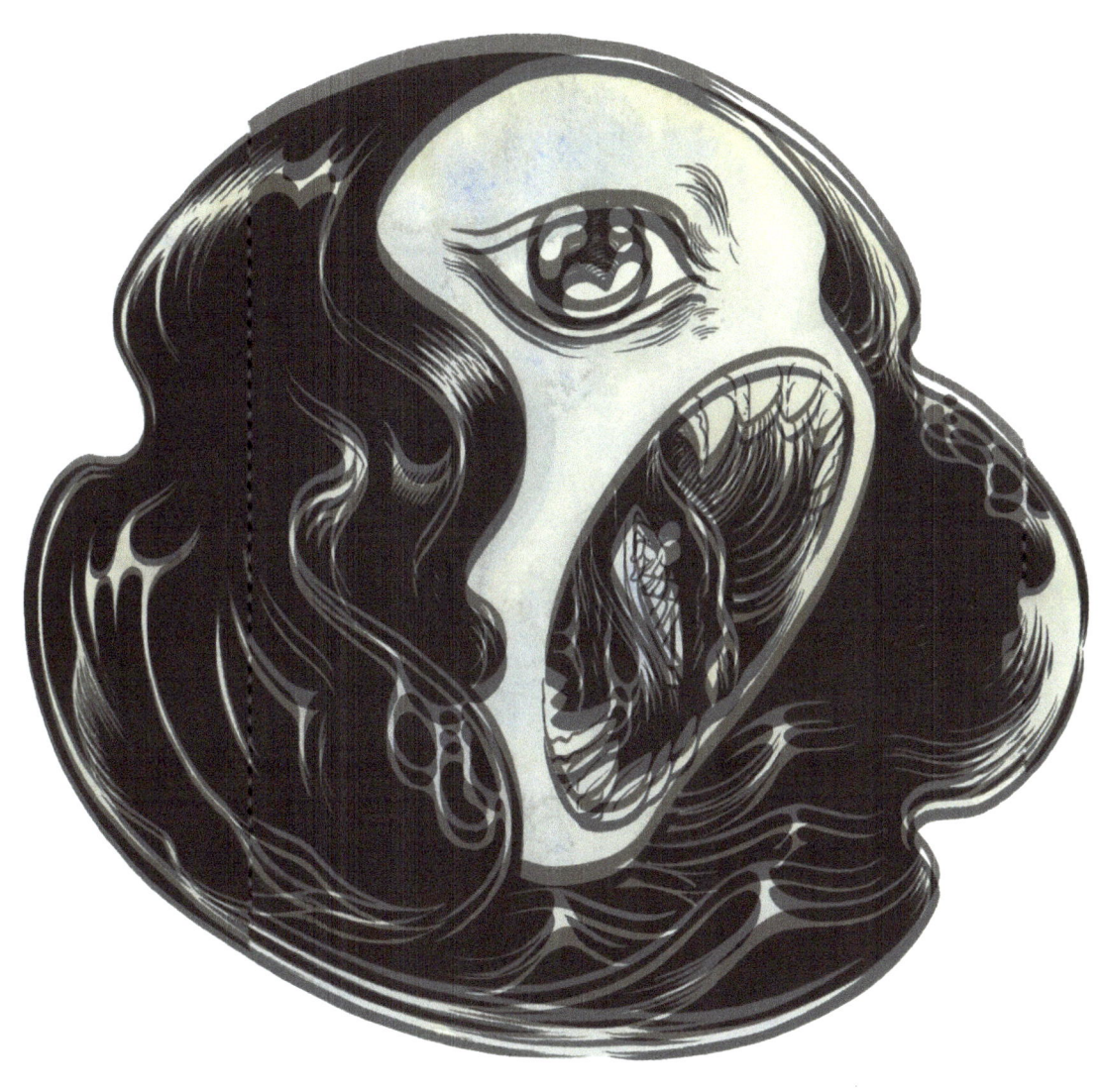

The Fly Catcher

My grandmother always said,

You catch more flies with honey.

So, whenever I was mad at you,

I'd be painfully sweet.

I'd imagine myself as some type of golden honey monster.

I would lather myself in honey from head-to-toe.

It would drip down my arms,

And cling to my hair.

It would ooze over my breasts,

And spew out of my mouth.

It would glaze over my eyes,

And seep into all my pores.

I would smother you with the honey from my palm,

and tear you open with my honey-coated teeth.

When it was all over,

I'd smile and admire just how many flies your hollowed out, honey-soaked carcass would collect.

Krysta Fitzpatrick

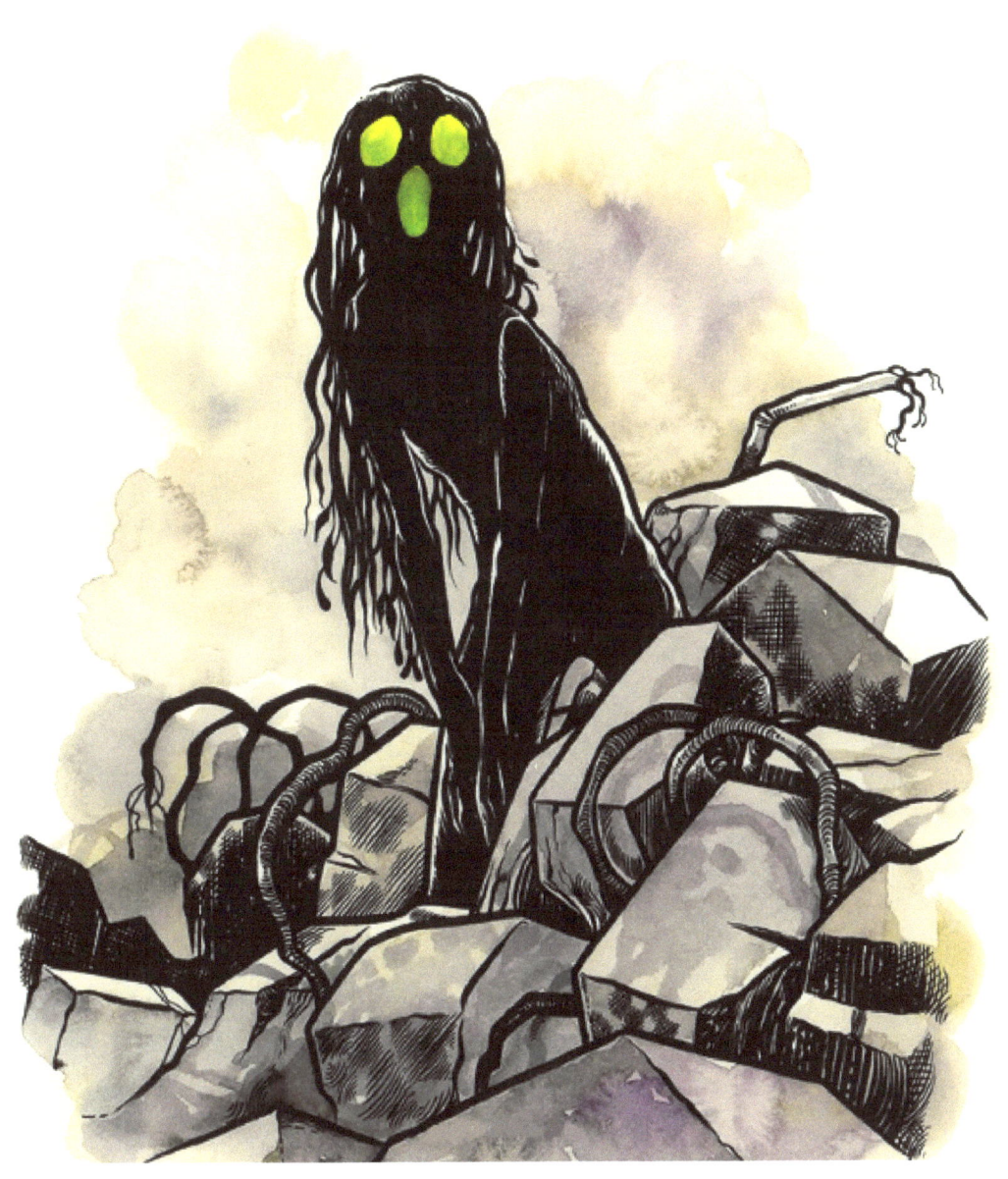

The Women with Fire in their Bellies

The Women with Fire in their Bellies is a collective of three prominent feminist poets from the island of Newfoundland. They include, in order of first publication, Hannah Jenkins, Samm Joyy, and Dr. Krysta Fitzpatrick. The collective is named for a line in Engen Books' first poetry collection, *The Birds Come Back in the Spring* by Hannah Jenkins.

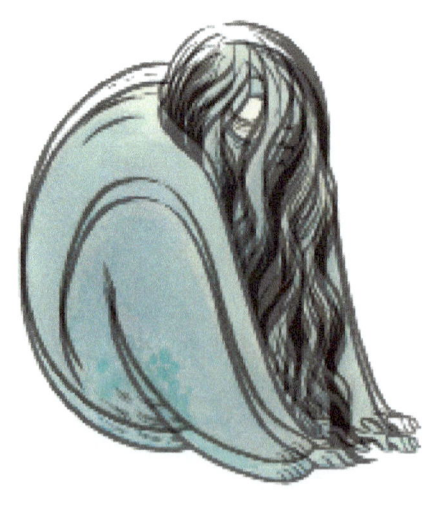

Krysta Fitzpatrick

Dr. Krysta Fitzpatrick is an educator and writer from St. John's, Newfoundland. She is currently teaching in both the English and Gender Studies Departments of Memorial University.

She resides in Mount Pearl with her husband, two sons, mother, and beloved dog Dipper.

Her debut collection, *The Vicious Kind*, was released in 2024.

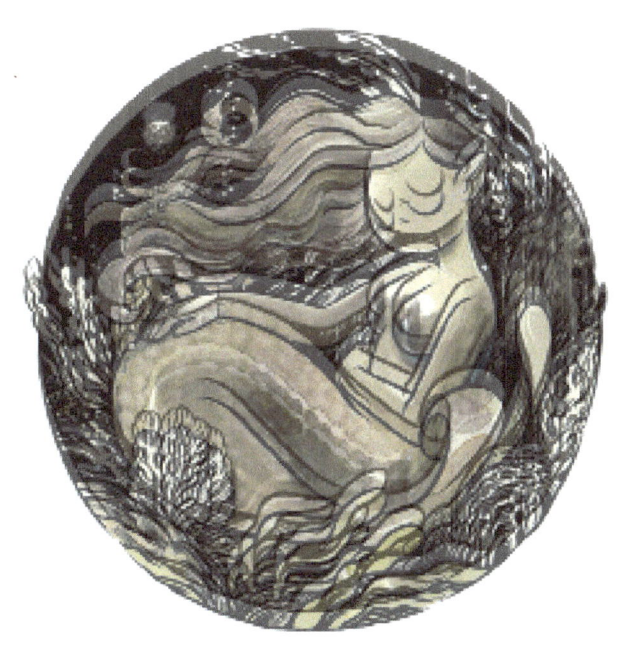

Hannah Jenkins

Hannah Jenkins is an author, artist, and library worker currently located in St. John's, Newfoundland and Labrador. She holds a Bachelor's Degree in English Literature and a Master's Degree in Applied Literary Arts. Her debut poetry collection, *The Birds Come Back in the Spring*, was published in 2022 through Engen Books and has remained a consistent bestseller for the company ever since.

Her work has appeared in various publications, including *Riddlefence, PRISM International, WORD magazine*, and more. Hannah has served as a Writer-in-Residence at the Corner Brook Public Library and is the current Youth Advocate for WritersNL. She is passionate about creating an inclusive and accessible literary community and has a particular interest in engaging with young and emerging writers as they begin their writing journeys.

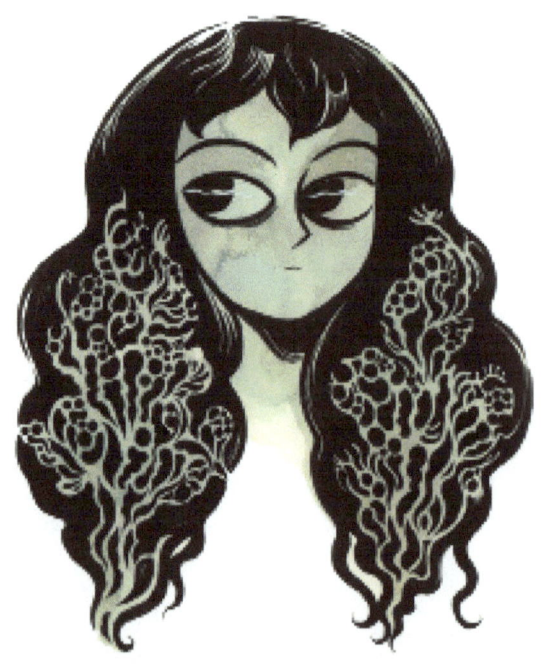

Samm Joyy

Samm Joyy is a poet born, raised, and living in St. John's, Newfoundland.

One of the most brilliant young authors of her time, Joyy helped run the Spoken Word St. John's (SWSJ) poetry scene from 2014-2022. In 2022 she edited *The Birds Come Back in the Spring*, the debut poetry collection from Hannah Jenkins.

Her poems focus on how one comes to grip with the darker aspects of one's own personality, grows to accept them, and eventually grows to feel comfortable showing them to the world. Her brutally honest work examines not only the poet but Newfoundland culture, touching on alcoholism, the arts, and downtown life.

Her debut collection, *A Decade*, was released in 2024.

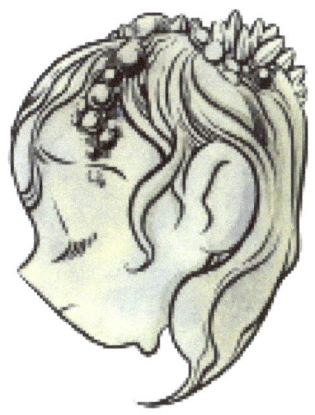

Kelly Bastow

Kelly Bastow is an illustrator and comic artist from Conception Bay South. She uses ink and watercolors to create her images, which often feature women, mythical creatures, and landscapes.

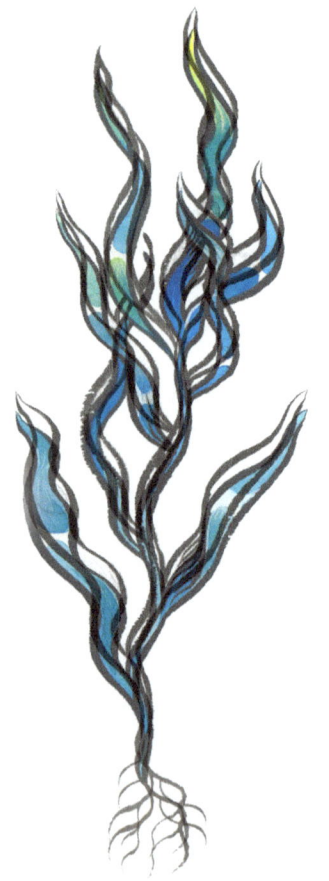
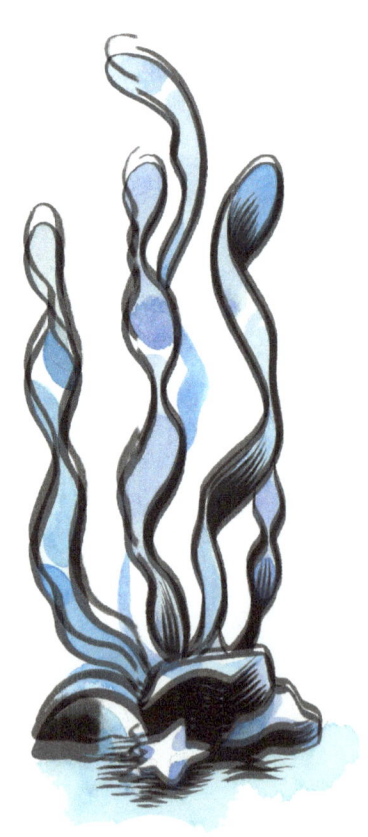

www.ingramcontent.com/pod-product-compliance
Lightning Source LLC
Chambersburg PA
CBHW051919210526
45473CB00006B/2069